Landmarks of world literature

Alexander Pushkin

EUGENE ONEGIN

Landmarks of world literature
General Editor: J. P. Stern

ALEXANDER PUSHKIN

Eugene Onegin

A. D. P. BRIGGS

*Professor of Russian Language and Literature,
University of Birmingham*

Published by the Press Syndicate of the University of Cambridge
The Pitt Building, Trumpington Street, Cambridge CB2 1RP
40 West 20th Street, New York NY 10011-4211, USA
10 Stamford Road, Oakleigh, Victoria 3166, Australia

First published 1992

Printed in Great Britain by Redwood Press Limited, Melksham, Wiltshire.

A catalogue record for this book is available from the British Library

Library of Congress cataloguing in publication data

Briggs, A. D. P.
Alexander Pushkin, Eugene Onegin / A. D. P. Briggs.
    p.   cm. – (Landmarks of world literature)
Includes bibliographical references.
ISBN 0 521 38472 9 (hardback)   ISBN 0 521 38618 7 (paperback)
1. Pushkin, Aleksandr Sergeevich, 1799–1837. Evgenii Onegin.
I. Title.   II. Series.
PG3343.E83B75   1992
891.71'3 – dc20   91-43489   CIP

ISBN 0 521 38472 9 hardback

WG

Contents

Preface

The most important event in the story of *Eugene Onegin* occurred at nine o'clock on the morning of 21 January 1821 when a boy of eighteen was shot dead in a duel. His victorious opponent was a mature man of twenty-five and an experienced duellist. The circumstances of the duel had been manipulated in the older man's favour. It was the offended party, Vladimir Lensky, who died − not the offender, Eugene Onegin.

The facts are clear. Onegin not only caused the duel, un-provoked, but carried it through ruthlessly, having been like a cheat and a murderer. Why, then, has he been treated so lightly by almost all the critics who have written about him? Why are they so ready to explain his conduct in terms of external cir-cumstances bearing upon him and diminishing his guilt? Why do some people even forget that a duel took place, believing that the unsuccessful relationship between Onegin and Tatyana is all that matters in this story? This book addresses these questions and, in view of the answers to them, attempts a reappraisal of all the main events and characters.

Eugene Onegin is not just a novel; it is a novel written in poetry of the highest quality. An explanation is given of the '*Onegin* stanza', and two such stanzas are examined in detail. Pushkin's role as a linguistic and literary innovator is also described.

Finally, this novel is placed in its literary-historical context. Drawing inspiration from writers as diverse as Sterne, Constant and Byron, and standing also at the head of the great tradition of nineteenth-century Russian realist fiction, *Eugene Onegin* may be seen to have emerged from, and contributed to, the mainstream of European culture. It is a true landmark in world literature.

Note on translations and references

In the first chapter, four complete stanzas of *Eugene Onegin* have been given in Charles Johnston's verse translation in order to give some idea to non-Russian speakers of the feel and flow of an *Onegin* stanza. Subsequently literal translations of passages under discussion have been supplied.

Extracts from the text are indicated by chapter and stanza number, e.g. (one, XX). Numerous references have been made to Vladimir Nabokov's literal translation and commentary; these indicate volume and page, e.g. (vol. 3, p. 41).

Chronology

	Pushkin's life and works	Related literary and historical events
1799	May 26: Aleksandr Sergeyevich Pushkin born Moscow.	Birth of Balzac
1800–11	Entrusted to nursemaids, French tutors and governesses, Pushkin grew up without parental affection. A lazy child, but an avid, precocious reader. Learned Russian from household serfs and especially his nanny, Arina Rodionovna.	
1801		Murder of Tsar Paul. Accession of Alexander I. Chateaubriand: *Atala.*
1802		Death of Radishchev, political radical, author of *A Journey from St Petersburg to Moscow.* Birth of Hugo. Mme de Staël: *Delphine.* Chateaubriand: *René.*
1803		Death of Bogdanovich, poet, author of *Dushen'ka.*
1804		Birth of George Sand. Death of Kant.
1805		Battles of Trafalgar and Austerlitz. Death of Schiller.
1807		Mme de Staël: *Corinne.*
1808		Scott: *Marmion.* Goethe: *Faust,* Part One.
1809		Birth of Gogol. Krylov: first book of Fables.
1810		Birth of Musset. Mme de Staël: *De l'Allemagne.*

	Pushkin's life and works	Related literary and historical events
1811		Zhukovsky: *Svetlana*. Austen: *Sense and Sensibility*. Byron: *Childe Harold's Pilgrimage*, Cantos One and Two. Birth of Belinsky, radical literary critic.
1811–17	Studied at the new lycée of Tsarskoye Selo, near St Petersburg	
1812		Napoleon's invasion of Russia. Battle of Borodino. Seizure of Moscow, followed by Napoleon's retreat.
1813		Austen: *Pride and Prejudice*. Byron: *The Giaour*.
1814		Paris taken by Allied Forces. Birth of Lermontov. Scott: *Waverley*.
1815		Battle of Waterloo. Holy Alliance initiated by Alexander I.
1816		Deaths of the poet Derzhavin and playwright Ozerov. Byron: *The Prisoner of Chillon*. Coleridge: *Christabel*. Constant: *Adolphe*. Goethe: *Italienische Reise*.
1817		Byron: *Manfred*. *Childe Harold's Pilgrimage*, final cantos.
1817–20	Occupied an undemanding government post in St Petersburg. Dissipated life style. Tenuous connections with revolutionary-minded young people. Some poems, unpublishable because of their liberal sentiments, circulated in manuscript form.	
1818		Birth of Turgenev. Death of satirical journalist Novikov. Byron: *Beppo*.

1819		Byron: *Don Juan*, Cantos One and Two. Stendhal: *De l'Amour*.
1820	March 26: completed *Ruslan and Lyudmila* after two years' work. May 6: exiled to Yekaterinoslav in the south. September 21: transferred to Kishinev, the capital of Bessarabia.	Lamartine: *Premières Méditations*. Shelley: *Prometheus Unbound*.
1820–1	*The Captive of the Caucasus.*	
1821	*The Robber Brothers.*	Births of Dostoyevsky, Baudelaire and Flaubert. Death of Keats.
1822	*The Fountain of Bakhchisaray.*	Death of Shelley.
1823	May 9: Began *Eugene Onegin*. July: transferred to Odessa. The last year of his four-year southern exile.	Lamartine: *Nouvelles Méditations*.
1824	Returned north to his parents' estate at Mikhaylovskoye. Two further years of exile. *The Gipsies.*	Byron: *Don Juan*, final cantos. Death of Byron. Griboyedov: *Woe from Wit*.
1825	*Count Nulin. Boris Godunov.*	Death of Alexander I. Accession of Nicholas I. Ruthless suppression of Decembrist uprising.
1825	September 8: freed from exile; summoned to Moscow by Nicholas I, who became his personal censor. Returned to dissipated life style.	Deaths of the poet and Decembrist leader Ryleyev (by execution) and Karamzin, writer, journalist and historian.
1827		Death of Blake. Manzoni: *I Promessi Sposi*.
1828	*Poltava.*	Birth of Leo Tolstoy.
1829	May–September: four-month visit to Transcaucasia, including action with the Russian army at war with the Turks.	Death of Griboyedov. Balzac: *Les Chouans*.
1830	September–November: stranded at his new estate of Boldino by an outbreak of cholera. *The Little House in Kolomna. The 'Little Tragedies'. The Tales of Belkin.*	Battle of *Hernani*.

	Pushkin's life and works	Related literary and historical events
1831	February 18: married to Natalya Goncharova. October 5: completed *Eugene Onegin* after more than eight years' writing.	Death of Hegel. Stendhal: *Le Rouge et le Noir*.
1832	May 19: birth of first child, Marya.	Goethe: *Faust*, Part Two. Death of Goethe. Death of Scott.
1833	Travelled east to the Urals, engaged in historical research. October–November: the second 'Boldino autumn'. *Andzhelo*. *The Bronze Horseman*. *The Queen of Spades*.	Heine: *Die romantische Schule*.
1833–5	*The Captain's Daughter*.	
1833–6	An unhappy period in St Petersburg; humiliation in court circles, jealousy of his wife's admirers, mounting debts. Little creative work.	
1834		Death of Coleridge.
1837	Goaded by scandalous rumours into a duel with Georges D'Anthès, an adopted son of the Dutch ambassador. The duel took place on January 27; Pushkin was wounded in the stomach and died two days later.	

Chapter 1

The poetry of *Eugene Onegin*

Introduction

Alexander Pushkin's *Eugene Onegin* is one of the most distinctive and significant of all the landmarks of world literature. It stands in a proud position at the very head of modern Russian literature, first-born in the grand series of nineteenth-century realist novels for which that culture is so highly esteemed. After Pushkin came Lermontov, Gogol, Turgenev, Dostoyevsky, Tolstoy and all the rest; without him as forebear they could never have written as they did. Any educated Russian will tell you that Pushkin is the father of their literature, even the creator of the modern literary Russian language; he or she will probably also add that *Eugene Onegin* is his greatest work. It is also a work which people love, savour and return to; a classic that they want to keep on reading. A measure of the affection in which this story is held may be taken from its unusual claim to be probably the most intimately known of all literary landmarks except for the Bible and the Koran. It is too good not to learn by heart. Russians do this, either under coercion at school or as a labour of love, and never regret it. Your present author would not have approached this book without having lived intimately with *Eugene Onegin* for years that run into decades and without committing large tracts of it to memory. To state this is not to show off; it is to pay due tribute in advance to one of the world's finest books and to mark its uniqueness. How many other such landmarks can inspire, and perhaps require, such intimate familiarity?

Another astonishing quality of *Eugene Onegin* is its length. How many famous novels are shorter? If you add up the words you will come to little more than 21,000, about half the length of this slender commentary. This makes Pushkin an interesting comparison with other nineteenth-century novelists, most of whom – certainly Dickens, Manzoni, Stendhal, Balzac, Tolstoy and Dostoyevsky – dole out their words in multiples of 100,000. Even Benjamin Constant, whose *Adolphe* is a byword for intense brevity, needed half as many words again as Pushkin does for *Onegin*.

The reason behind the memorability and sheer density of this work is not far to seek. It is a novel written in poetry – a further claim to uniqueness; other attempts have been made in this direction, but not a single unqualified success has been recorded beyond *Eugene Onegin*. And the poetry is of singular quality, written by an unequalled master in the springtime of Russian verse so that every word, rhyme and trope is resplendent with newness and spontaneity. Although the novel contains much that is fascinating in the way of character, incident and serious ideas, the poetry simply cannot be ignored. A recent study of the novel ran to 234 large pages without any discussion of it; this was a mistake and it led to some wrong conclusions, particularly in exaggerating the sombre melancholy of the novel. Poetic quality ought to be the first and the last impression gained from *Eugene Onegin*.

Poetry should be considered in relation to the language in which it is written and it is with the Russian language that our study must begin. The nature of that language, the radical transformation of it by this one writer and the qualities which set it apart from other European tongues – these topics form a necessary preliminary to the main discussion. They will, incidentally, help us to understand some of the difficulties faced by translators into English verse.

The Russian Language

Modern Russian is a particularly pleasing language to hear and to speak. It derives from an oral East Slavonic dialect and from Old Church Slavonic, the first written language of the Slavs, artificially created in the ninth century for Christian Church purposes and with a strong input of Greek. Over several centuries it was enriched by further infusions of German, Dutch, English and particularly French. Numerous words of oriental origin have also crept in. Russian now emerges as a most expressive language, with an uncommonly wide range of sounds and a huge lexicon. In the hands of the right practitioner it can be made to sound as mellifluous as operatic Italian or as vigorous as anything from northern Europe. Much energy and colour derive from its strong, variable word stress and also from rich consonantal clustering. As an inflected language it tends towards long, polysyllabic words and it enjoys considerable freedom of word order — objects can precede subjects without ambiguity because the grammatical function of most words is indicated by changed endings. It is complicated rather than intrinsically difficult. Russians are naturally proud of such a tongue and frequently speak of its virtues. Ivan Turgenev summed up its quality, and also Alexander Pushkin's role in its formation, in a famous speech of 1880. Pushkin, he explained, 'gave a final form to our language, which in richness, strength, logic and beauty is acknowledged even by foreign philologists to be inferior only perhaps to that of Ancient Greece.'

Even as late as the beginning of the nineteenth century the language was still in bits and pieces. French was spoken and read on all decorous occasions and Russian itself existed in several different forms, archaic, Gallicised, everyday workmanlike and crudely vulgar. A century earlier educated people had been encouraged to stratify the language, differentiating between its various uses, and these habits had been only partly eroded. Pushkin's achievement was to unify all the disparate linguistic forces. He began to write in a new language, for which any vocabulary and syntax could be mobilised, from the most exalted to the humblest and crudest. All that was needed was a fine enough sensitivity to ensure that the expression exactly suited the occasion. Pretentiousness, false shame and hypocrisy went out of the door; in through the window came a spirit of cultural emancipation and democracy. The language, already massively enriched, now lost its shackles and ran away free. Pushkin was its liberator and its first creative practitioner.

The newness of the language accounts for one of the brightest features of *Eugene Onegin*, its sense of purity and freshness. The novel is beset with dismal stories of staleness, depression, disappointment, frustration and even dark tragedy; it is paradoxical that such material should be presented in a manner which actually invigorates and inspires. Perhaps only Shakespeare (as in *Romeo and Juliet*, for example) may be said to have been a better master at telling sad tales with such a poetic touch that their awfulness is transmuted into a sense of beauty.

It must not be thought that Pushkin set about consciously to reform his native language. What happened was instinctive. He was the most natural and spontaneous of writers who sensed no obstacles or boundaries when he wrote. His Russian is by turns colloquial, neutrally descriptive or discursive, mischievously humorous, fiendishly sharp, highly coloured, sublime and rhetorical. It can go anywhere and do anything. Its greatest quality is the one you notice least, unless you listen very closely − sheer aptness. Simply by writing the right words in the right order, and having no difficulty in doing so, Alexander Pushkin raised high the status of Russian, proved once and for all that, as the most attractive and expressive of all the European languages, it need fear no other − French least of all − and invited his successors to use it with unassailable confidence. They did not let him down.

Problems of translation

Translating this remarkable language is no easy matter. Russian and English are distant cousins within the Indo-European family and they share some similarities, such as complex origins and strong primary word stress. Nevertheless, they stand far apart. Russian has the greater acoustic opulence, much longer words and more freedom in deploying their order. English, on the other hand, has a sense of uncluttered exactitude, a delicacy of expression and an even broader range of vocabulary available for the refinement of meaning. It has been calculated that in an average passage of English which includes some dialogue almost eighty per cent of the words used are likely

to be monosyllabic (Scherr, *Russian Poetry*, p. 5); this gives
our language a punchy style that Russian does not aspire to.

In the translation of most prose texts these differences may
be said not to matter very much. In poetry they certainly do.
Alexander Pushkin's beautifully judged poetic Russian is particularly vulnerable to misrepresentation. Whatever you do with
it in English it will sound very different, and usually wrong.
Of all his works *Eugene Onegin* has suffered most by failures
in translation, not merely because no first-class poet has ever
tackled the job, but because it is literally impossible to come
anywhere near to success in this enterprise.

First, the line length. More will be said soon about the
Onegin stanza. For the moment it is enough to note that the
five thousand lines of this novel are all iambic tetrameters.
This eight- or nine-syllable line accommodates the Russian
language well. Its four feet readily accept an average of four
words, though the incidence of actual two-syllable words is
low. The charm of the line in its multiple use arises from the
interplay between the many assertive words of three syllables
or more and the subversive little words which prevent them
from achieving total domination. You cannot help but notice
the long words; everything is going for them — size, spread
and sound. They sprawl across the line, self-confident, eye-
catching: words like *zakonodatel'*, *prichudnitsy*, *poluzhivogo*,
vdokhnovitel'noy, *madrigal'nykh*, *schastliveyshiye* and so on.
What is less apparent is that they are interpenetrated by fussy
little prepositions, pronouns, short forms and other modest
elflike words which provide variety and create a happy balance
of authority. For reasons difficult to determine, this ongoing
struggle, resolving itself repeatedly in the average distribution
of four Russian words over every four poetic feet, turns out
to be immensely satisfying. In English almost the opposite
occurs. If we have a favourite line of verse it is clearly the
iambic pentameter, so that our language, with its much shorter
words, ironically demands a longer line. It is not easy to understand why. Perhaps we derive our enjoyment from the scurry-
ing around of small words as they find their obedient places in
a capacious line, fighting off the domination of the occasional

bullying long word. Of course it can work in reverse. Russian can produce a monosyllabic line such as 'I tam ya byl, i med ya pil' ('And I was there and I drank mead') (Pushkin's *Ruslan i Lyudmila*); conversely English is capable of a grand locution such as 'The multitudinous seas incarnadine' (*Macbeth*). But, by and large, there can be no doubting the Russian preference for long words in a short line, with a reversal of that in English.

What happens when we translate from Russian to English? The answer is that we inevitably substitute our own syllabic patterns for theirs. This unfortunate process can be quantified. Take the opening stanza of *Eugene Onegin*. In Russian it contains sixty-one words, slightly above the average for the whole poem which is nearer to fifty-eight per stanza. In half a dozen English translations, written over a century between 1881 and 1977, the totals for this stanza vary from eighty-one to ninety-two words and average out at eighty-seven. From sixty-one to eighty-seven is a massive jump, the order of forty-three per cent. One translator, Oliver Elton, raises the number of words by almost precisely fifty per cent. This is no incidental variation; it is a tangible measure by which we can watch Pushkin's poetry draining away in translation.

A single example may be taken to demonstrate the steady process by which Pushkin is traduced by his translators. In the twentieth stanza of *Eugene Onegin* (which will soon be discussed in detail) there occurs a lovely line consisting of only two words, separated by a comma. The ballerina Istomina is described as *Blistatel'na, poluvozdushna*, which means 'Resplendent, half-ethereal'. Unfortunately the translators have not been able to use any such phrase in their versions. This exquisite bivalve of a line is split up and broken down in English. Here are some examples: 'Brilliant, ethereal, there springs...' (1881), 'A fairy light about her playing ...' (sic) (1936), 'And there, resplendent, in the middle...' (1937), 'There stands ashimmer, half ethereal...' (1963), 'Then with a half-ethereal splendour...' (1977). Even when the line succeeds as poetry, it is not Pushkin's poetry. This example is a striking one, but it illustrates what happens continually to Pushkin when he is forced through the filter between Russian and English. What begins as a series of magical and musical tetrameters in his native tongue often ends up like English children's doggerel.

The question of single versus double rhymes makes things even worse. This problem is insoluble; whichever way you settle it you do harm to the original. Because of its long words and many inflexions the Russian language has no trouble in digging up masses of double (or feminine) rhymes, those of two syllables, such as (in English) 'season/reason'. It is common for the poet to alternate these with single (masculine) rhymes, such as 'gown/frown'. Pushkin does so throughout *Eugene Onegin* and the appetising rhythmic pulse of the *Onegin* stanza depends upon this alternation. How shall the translator react to it? A poisoned chalice awaits on either hand. If he does not look for feminine rhymes in English he will reconstruct the stanza and misrepresent it in rhythmic terms. But the regular use of double rhymes in English is probably even worse. Although the rhythm stays approximately the same, the translator has to do what no English poet (other than a humorist) would dream of doing. He has to force our language to yield up rhymes which are so hackneyed ('ocean/motion'), or feeble ('calling/falling'), or outrageously eye-catching ('misrepresent them/Bentham') that they ruin Pushkin's effects of delicate and appropriate rhyming. There is no way out of this impasse; you end up either with a staccato stanza or with Gilbertian rhymes.

There are other obstacles to adequate translation, but these are the main stumbling blocks. Every single translator has stumbled; it must be accepted by the non-Russian speaking world that no real impression of this work will ever be gained from reading it in translation. This does not mean that the seven or eight valiant attempts already made are negligible. They have a number of uses. At least an outline of the events and characters in *Eugene Onegin* may be discerned in even the weakest of them, and this will be of use to those non-Russian speakers who wish to know more about the flow of European literature. Opera lovers, approaching *Eugene Onegin* via Tchaikovsky's version (a lovely experience in itself, but unPushkinian in its Romantic sentimentality) may wish to read the source novel out of curiosity. The right thing to do is, of course, to learn Russian; those who are part way through that process might well use a translation, for all its perfidy, as a helpful crib. A special word must be said about the celebrated four-volume translation and commentary by Vladimir Nabokov. Despite its excellence this will be of little use to those without Russian. The doggedly literal translation is idiosyncratic and uninspiring; the cornucopian notes are a treat for those who wish to extend an already existing knowledge of the novel.

The *Onegin* stanza

In his serious narrative poetry, of which there is a great deal, Pushkin always avoids using stanzas. They are too constraining and too self-consciously poetic for his free-running narrative style. For his novel in verse, however, he did revert to stanzas; they are its distinguishing feature in terms of form. He did so only because the particular stanza invented for the occasion proved to have most unusual properties. The *Onegin* stanza, as it turned out, was able to provide a strong skeletal form for the novel, guaranteeing shapeliness, discipline and dignified stature. At the same time it possessed an inner flexibility capable of producing simultaneously almost the opposite impression – mercurial movement and inexhaustible plasticity. This paradox of form needs explaining.

The *Onegin* stanza is actually an adaptation of the sonnet. That in itself is an excellent start; we all know that this hallowed form is capable of great things. It is of an appropriate length to accommodate and develop to the full at least one serious idea; it also knows when enough is enough. The entire feel of the sonnet form is wholesome, telling in advance of serious purposes, beauty, strength and proportion. It even looks good on the page. If it has a fault it is that the sonnet is a short, intense form that stands alone; it does not seem to be adaptable for narrative purposes. But all Pushkin wanted was the outline and the general feel of this special form. For his purposes he had every intention of altering it. First, he shortened the line. Most sonnets are written in pentameters; he was not going to go beyond his beloved tetrameter. More importantly, he devised a new rhyme scheme which proved to be a miracle of inventiveness. This needs looking at in detail.

The scheme goes as follows (using capital letters to indicate the double rhymes):

A b A b C C d d E f f E g g

Clearly the stanza consists of three differently formed quatrains followed by a couplet. The English, or Shakespearean, sonnet goes like that (though the quatrains are usually more regular). The argument of the words used is taken progressively through three stages and is rounded off, or underlined, or subverted (or whatever else) in a snappy terminal couplet. Thus Pushkin's variant should apparently be construed as:

(A b A b) + (C C d d) + (E f f E) + (g g)

In *Eugene Onegin* there are a number of stanzas in which the sense of the words does move along according to that pattern. A good example may be seen in the stanza XLVIII of chapter one (given here in Russian followed by Charles Johnston's translation).

1	С душою, полной сожалений,	A
2	И опершися на гранит,	b
3	Стоял задумчиво Евгений,	A
4	Как описал себя Пиит.	b
5	Все было тихо; лишь ночные	C
6	Перекликались часовые;	C
7	Да дрожек отдаленный стук	d
8	С Мильонной раздавался вдруг;	d
9	Лишь лодка, веслами махая,	E
10	Плыла по дремлющей реке;	f
11	И нас пленяли вдалеке	f
12	Рожок и песня удалая ...	E
13	Но слаще, средь ночных забав,	g
14	Напев Торкватовых октав!	g

1	Evgeny stood, with soul regretful,	A
2	And leant upon the granite shelf;	b
3	He stood there, pensive and forgetful,	A
4	Just as the poet paints himself.	b

5	Silence was everywhere enthralling;	C
6	Just sentries to each other calling,	C
7	And then a drozhky's clopping sound	d
8	From Million Street came floating round;	d
9	And then a boat, with oars a-swinging,	E
10	Swam on the river's dreaming face,	f
11	And then, with an enchanting grace,	f
12	Came distant horns, and gallant singing.	E
13	Yet sweeter far, at such a time,	g
14	The strain of Tasso's octave-rhyme!	g

The neatness of this 'English' 'sonnet' is exemplary. All three quatrains are sealed hermetically with a full-stop or at least a semi-colon; the final couplet crowns its confident individuality with an exclamation mark. All four sections present slightly different, though elated, ideas. The first quatrain (lines 1–4) gives us a picture of Eugene leaning on the river parapet. The second one (lines 5–8) describes certain sounds which float across the night air. The third one (lines 9–12) depicts a boat on the sleepy water of the river, and calls up more sounds from even further away. These twelve lines add up to a delectable picture of the night scene, expressed in some of Pushkin's loveliest poetry. The last couplet is surprisingly different. The poet says that, despite the beauty of the present scene, he would really like to be somewhere else. By referring to Tasso he is telling us that he would prefer to be alongside one of the canals of Venice listening to a gondolier. It turns out that this couplet, which gives a naughty twist to the end of stanza XLVIII, is merely a prelude to reflexions on his wish to leave Russia and visit Italy, all of which takes up stanza XLIX. The whole job is beautifully done, the poet having exhausted the full potential of this particular 'sonnet' form.

But poets want more than to repeat earlier successes. John Keats, for instance, was not satisfied with his own ability to write sonnets of one particular kind. In 1818, sensing an early death, he wrote the moving sonnet, 'When I have fears that I may cease to be...' for which he too used the 'English' variety, though with a simpler rhyme scheme (a b a b c d c d e f e f g g). This makes an interesting comparison with that earlier sonnet of his, *On First Looking into Chapman's Homer* (1816), with

its well-known opening, 'Much have I travelled in the realms
of gold ...' This follows quite a different form, the rhyme-
scheme being a b b a a b b a c d c d c d. In this kind of sonnet,
known as the 'Italian' or 'Petrarchan', the fourteen lines are
differently grouped. A strong pause in the sense is required
after the eighth line and the stanza breaks into two unequal
parts, an octave and a sestet. It is important for there to be
two distinct ideas in the poem, one for each 'half'; in Keats's
case the octave of the *Chapman's Homer* sonnet describes the
poet's earlier inability to sense the spirit of Homer, despite
visiting his land, and the sestet puts things right by explaining
how Chapman has transformed his vision. Keats, then, is able
to use the two distinct sonnet forms at will, and always with
an exact sense of appropriateness.

Alexander Pushkin possesses the same skill, but with this
difference; he can do it within a single work. The remarkable
property of the *Onegin* stanza is that it can bend itself into
either (or any) of the main sonnet forms. The secret lies in the
third quatrain, lines 9, 10, 11 and 12, which form an envelope
E ff E preceding the final couplet g g. It is clear that these six
lines could be divided up in two different ways to form either
a 3 + 3 group (E ff + E g g) or a 4 + 2 group (E ff E + g g).
We have seen the latter grouping at work in an 'English'
stanza. All that has to happen is that the wording of the last
six lines should involve a break *one line earlier* (after E ff) and
we have the makings of the other potential sonnet form, the
Italian. This will occur in its pure form if line 8 also ends
strongly. To make the matter clearer let us look at such a stanza.
A good example (on an appropriate subject, the study of the
Classics) occurs in one, VIII:

1	Латынь из моды вышла ныне:	A
2	Так, если правду вам сказать,	b
3	Он знал довольно по-латыни,	A
4	Чтоб эпиграфы разбирать,	b
5	Потолковать об Ювенале,	C
6	В конце письма поставить *vale*,	C
7	Да помнил, хоть не без греха,	d
8	Из Энеиды два стиха.	d

9	Он рыться не имел охоты	E
10	В хронологической пыли	f
11	Бытописания земли:	f
12	Но дней минувших анекдоты	E
13	От Ромула до наших дней	g
14	Хранил он в памяти своей.	g

1	Now Latin's gone quite out of favour;	A
2	Yet, truthfully, and not in chaff,	b
3	Onegin knew enough to savour	A
4	The meaning of an epigraph,	b
5	Make Juvenal his text, or better	C
6	Add *vale* when he signed a letter;	C
7	Stumblingly call to mind he did	d
8	Two verses of the Aeneid.	d
9	He lacked the slightest predilection	E
10	For raking up historic dust	f
11	Or stirring annalistic must;	f
12	But groomed an anecdote collection	E
13	That stretched from Romulus in his prime	g
14	Across the years to our own time.	g

Note that the only two full-stops mark clearly the end of the octave (line 8) and of the sestet (line 14). Note also the strong semi-colon break at the end of line 11; this muscular thrust single-handedly reshapes the ending into a palpable E ff + E gg form. The stanza has assumed the following shape:

$$((A\ b\ A\ b) + (C\ C\ d\ d)) + ((E\ f\ f) + (E\ g\ g))$$

What must be borne in mind is that nothing has happened to the rhyme-scheme itself; this remains unchanged throughout all three hundred and sixty-six stanzas of *Eugene Onegin*. The point is that this rhyme-scheme *has no inbuilt predisposition to one sonnet form or another*. By changing the pauses and breaks it can assume any desired 'sonnet' form. (It can even parody its origin by playfully putting the sestet before the octave, as in one, X). The first unusual property of the *Onegin* stanza is, therefore, its friendly tractability. It does not mind being taken anywhere; it will put on any disguise. Linked with this pliable geniality is a sense of mystery. Even when you know the stanza intimately it remains exceedingly difficult to find your way through it without losing your sense of direction.

This strange quality of disorientation emanates from the middle and later sections which, despite the predictability of the rhyme scheme, always remain a puzzle and a problem. It is a curious property of this stanza that in among the rigidly predetermined rhyming groups there are *three* occasions when *three successive lines do not rhyme together*. Here is the scheme with the relevant sections underlined:

A b A b C C d d E f f E g g

The first of these presents little or no problem. The opening quatrains of the *Onegin* stanza are always rock solid. A huge proportion of them − probably near to three quarters of them all − are so self-sustaining that they end in a full-stop or near equivalent (a question mark, exclamation mark or at least a semi-colon). Thus at all times it is quite clear what is happening when this first quatrain ends and the next one begins. The A and b rhymes complete those deposited two lines earlier and there is no mystery in the occurrence of a C rhyme; it is needed to start the next sequence. There is a little moment of surprise when line 6 repeats the C, because we were vaguely anticipating another alternating quatrain, in which case C d C d would have occurred. But matters are soon put right. By the end of line 8 we can see that two different kinds of quatrain have been set down. On into the middle of the stanza. Here the second and third unrhymed triplets cannot be swallowed so easily. In the space of six lines (8−13) four different rhymes are used and it is not easy to tell what they are doing. As you wander through this territory you cannot readily grasp whether the line you are in is going to clinch a rhyme already established or open up a new one. The shapes and the relationships are blurred. This must be confusing for newcomers to the stanza, but they should be reassured by the fact that even those who have read the novel many times and know whole tracts of it by heart feel the same sense of disorientation at this point. It is not a mistake, deficiency or drawback. On the contrary, this shiftiness is deliberately infused into the basic stanza so that it will always beguile and entertain rather than yield its secrets readily. When critics use adjectives like 'protean', 'mercurial' or 'ever-changing' (which they often do in relation both to *Eugene Onegin* and to Pushkin's work as a whole), they are speaking in general terms of what we can now see demonstrated specifically.

Incidentally, full comprehension of the rich quality of the *Onegin* stanza can be achieved only by considering some of the alternatives. To take a contemporary example, Byron preferred to use *Ottava Rima* not only in a poem like *Beppo* but even in a long narrative like *Don Juan*. This consists of a simple, rigid and predictable formula, which runs ababab cc. The single advantage of this tedious grouping is that its user can play upon the reader's expectations to display his prowess as a rhymster. Thus Byron will set up a line-ending with the word 'intellectual' knowing that his readers will worry themselves silly about the rhyming possibilities and then smite hip and thigh when he comes up with 'henpecked you all' (*Don Juan*, one, XXII). This is genuinely amusing but not the sort of thing that Pushkin had the slightest interest in. As to the Spenserian stanza of *Childe Harold's Pilgrimage* (ababbcbdd), this amounts to an ongoing intellectual exercise, or a virtuoso display of intricate rhyming, which may amaze and delight for a stanza or two but which will probably dishearten most readers after a while through its repetitive insistency. True, the stanza possesses an admirable quality in its asymmetricality, but that is undermined every time by the use of four 'b' rhymes within six lines – and this in every single stanza. (Let us remember that in the *Onegin* stanza Pushkin uses four *different* rhymes in six successive lines.) Byron, incidentally, penned five hundred such stanzas in this poem and two thousand *Ottava Rima* ones in *Don Juan*, whereas Pushkin, it will bear repeating, wrote three hundred and sixty-six beautiful pseudo-sonnets in *Eugene Onegin*.

So much for specifics. A more general impression of how the *Onegin* stanza works may be gained from a nice metaphor created by Nabokov. He likens it to a painted ball which allows its patterns to be discerned at the start and end of its movement but which blurs them in mid-spin. The only weakness of this expressive idea is that it leaves the reader as a passive on-looker. A more useful metaphor, since it involves the reader in the action, might be that of a sea voyage out and home again. A leisurely departure occurs in the first quatrain where every-thing remains reassuringly dependable and the landmarks are familiar (AbAb). Then the going gets a little rough in the next one where some unexpected turbulence occurs (CCdd). The storm which is brewing here sets in properly in the third quatrain, where the terra firma of the opening one has been lost over the horizon and there is a real sense of not knowing where you are (EffE). Then suddenly the storm is over and the concluding couplet (gg) brings both relief and surprise. Without knowing quite how it happened, the traveller has been set down back home on familiar territory.

Anyone who has read, or listened to, a succession of these beautiful verses will be familiar with the movement described here. Particularly noticeable are the sense of smooth departure and the comforting feeling of reassurance which occur at the beginning and the end of virtually every stanza.

A close look at two stanzas

This, then, is the *Onegin* stanza, a remarkable invention by any poetic standards. But it is only a skeleton; it has to be fleshed and clothed. Full of potential it may be, but a mediocre poet could easily misuse it. We need now to move from the abstract to the particular by looking closely at a couple of actual stanzas in order to see how a first-rate poet brings out the best in his cleverly chosen form. It is surprisingly true that almost any stanzas would do for this purpose, but two especially rewarding ones from the first chapter offer themselves readily for analysis. Without seeming to add much to the story itself, they both present, in different ways, poetry of such heart-stopping quality that it calls out for explanation.

The first stanza (one, XX), is remembered for its description of the theatre, the ballet and specifically a noted ballerina of the day, Avdotiya Istomina, who is depicted first in a beauti-ful static pose, then in balletic movement. There is probably no more succinctly accurate depiction of this art anywhere in the world's literature than in this single evocative stanza.

> Театр уж полон; ложи блещут;
> Партер и кресла – все кипит;
> В райке нетерпеливо плещут,
> И, взвившись, занавес шумит.
> Блистательна, полувоздушна,
> Смычку волшебному послушна,
> Толпою нимф окружена,
> Стоит Истомина; она,
> Одной ногой касаясь пола,
> Другою медленно кружит,
> И вдруг прыжок, и вдруг летит,
> Летит, как пух от уст Эола,
> То стан совьет, то разовьет,
> И быстрой ножкой ножку бьет.

> The house is packed out; scintillating,
> The boxes; boiling pit and stalls;
> The gallery claps – it's bored with waiting –
> And up the rustling curtain crawls.
> Then with a half-ethereal splendour,
> Bound where the magic bow will send her
> Istomina, thronged all around
> By Naiads, one foot on the ground,
> Twirls the other slowly as she pleases,
> Then suddenly she's off, and there,
> She's up and flying through the air
> Like fluff before Aeolian breezes;
> She'll spin this way and that, and beat
> Against each other swift, small feet.

Pushkin's celebrated capacity for detailed miniaturisation is at work here. Looking back over the stanza one is amazed at how much detail there is. A whole world, with an entire population, has been encompassed within it. There are three distinct sections. The first four lines are brilliant, bustling and noisy; eighteen words tell a busy tale. The next four are quite the opposite, visual, quiet and static. This is the slender waist of the stanza; it has no more than eleven words (only one of which is a verb and that means nothing more energetic than 'she stands'). The last six lines describe movement, beginning from nothing, developing with exquisite slowness and then bursting into flight with the lightest touch imaginable. A lot of words (by Pushkin's economical standards) are needed; nineteen in the quatrain and a further ten in the final couplet. In all fifty-eight words are employed, which strikes the exact average per stanza for the whole novel. This needs some emphasis. Pushkin is working in paragraphs of fewer than sixty words, yet in each one he uses his poetic skills to impart large amounts of information, description or comment. The succinctness of this method is one of the remarkable features of his work and particularly of *Eugene Onegin*.

Let us look at some of the detail. In the opening quatrain our story-teller decides that the best way to evoke the atmosphere of the theatre just before a performance is to send us right round the building. We are given the best seats in the house, in the front centre of the dress circle; only from there can you see all that is now described. We are directed first to look across at the boxes, then down front at the pit, then down rear at the stalls, then up at the gods and finally at the stage itself to which we are drawn by the raising of the curtain. As if the eye did not have enough to do taking in this broad scene, the busy brilliance of it all is enhanced by the noises to which our ear is also directed; seething movement and conversation from below, restless handclapping from above, then the noisy swishing of the curtain. This latter action comes in the fourth line which is little short of miraculous in its poetic achievement. Full of movement and sound, it is overtly onomatopoeic but in an unusual way. The curious thing is that the actual onomatopoeic word *shumit* plays only a modest part in the sound pattern, coming as it does at the end of the line when most of the excitement is over. It is the remarkable word *vzvivshis'* that does most of the work and, strange though it may seem, this word is *not* intrinsically onomatopoeic. The word *vzvit'* simply means 'to raise': etymologically it has no connexion with sound, deriving as it does from the verb *vit'*, to wind or twist, and the prefix *vos* or *vz* which indicates ascension. By the wonderful anfractuosities of Russian grammar this energetic little root can be changed into something really

striking in terms of its sounds. You have to use the verb reflex-
ively and proceed through its various forms until you get to
the remotest of all, the past tense gerund. The clever part is to
select precisely this form, with its three v's in the first five letters
and a powerful combination of sibilants, z, sh and s, to follow
on, in order to describe the raising of a theatre curtain. It is
all downhill from now on. The poet can capitalise on the
sheer luck − Serendipity rather than Sergeyevich being
Alexander Pushkin's middle name − that the very Russian
word for curtain, *zanaves*, recapitulates three of these four
strong consonants, z, v and s. After that it is the work of a
moment to throw in the only obvious acoustic device, that
noisy word *shumit*, which normally demands for itself a proud
position in the sentence but here sulks at the line-end, looking
modest and even skimpy after what has gone before. Once
created this line looks natural, even inevitable. But how complex and unpredictable it really is. What nonsense it makes of
the very idea of translation. Before taking our leave of it let
us remind ourselves of the long succession of consonantal
explosions which accompany the raising of that curtain; they
go like this: v, z, v, v, sh, s, z, n, v, s, sh, m, t.

But we are only at line 4; there are more delights to come.
After the commotion, the visual and aural splendour of the
opening quatrain, we are ready for something different. We
did not come to the theatre to watch the crowd or the curtain.
What we now want are stillness, concentration, beauty and
the build-up of lovely movement, precisely what most of the
audience (though not, incidentally, Eugene himself) have come
to see. The contrast now introduced by line 5, and sustained for
precisely one more quatrain, is remarkable for its appropriateness and its aesthetic impact. A close look will show that, if
line 4 was unusual, line 5 is unique. It consists of two adjectives, each taking up half of the line. This itself is obvious,
but the hidden truth behind it is rather surprising. The line
looks peculiarly symmetrical on the page:

Блистательна, полувоздушна,

Such pleasing equilibrium, particularly after the seething tur-moil of what went before, derives from the fact that each half-line consists precisely of twelve printed signs. This is probably the only line in five thousand which divides itself with such exactitude, and it is called up at precisely the right moment in order to evoke in advance the spirit of Istomina. Perfectly poised, with dignity intact and unassailable, it takes up its own beautifully balletic stance; the ballerina is here before she has been named. The naming of her is itself, incidentally, delightfully done. You do not hurry these things. We are made to wait and grow in impatience just as the noisy crowd in the gods had to do. All the information about her comes first: 'Resplendent, half-ethereal, obedient to the magical bow, sur-rounded by a crowd of nymphs, there stands ... Istomina'. The gentle emphasis here imparted to her revered name, the relief which comes with its eventual utterance, these lovely feelings are the result of perfect timing on our story-teller's part; he has seen fit to hold back the name that matters until the tenth position in an eleven-word sequence. There is even a good reason for it not to be in eleventh place. As the all-important line sits on the page

Стоит Истомина; она

the goddess may be seen adopting a central stance surrounded on each side by modest (two-syllable) minions rather as she does on the stage itself surrounded by the nymphs. This minor point is hardly fanciful or without significance. Transposition of the last two words, which is grammatically possible, would erode the perfection of the line. Equilibrium is all that matters in this section of the poem. It is what Istomina represents; she is perfectly balanced under all conditions, whether she is standing (as in line 5), jumping or flying (line 11), or twisting and turning (line 13). All the poetic devices must come together and work towards a continuous reflexion of that quality. Following the line in which she is named, there are six more lines to come. Within them there are, appropriately, six different examples of syntactical parallelism. First the words *Odnoy* and *Drugoy* ('The one ...', 'The other ...') stand strongly at the beginning of lines 9 and 10, drawing attention to the delicately balanced contrast which we are observing. Then the slowness of the initial pirouette is set against the later rapidity of Istomina's entrechat. Here Pushkin rides his customary luck. The Russian word for 'slow' is a slow one and the Russian word for 'fast' is fast. So by using the normal words, *medlenno* and *bystro*, he automatically retards and hastens the action just as the moment demands; *medlenno* with its lingering double consonant is especially effective. Again, the contrast is palpable. So indeed are those in lines 11 and 13, both of which emulate the overt symmetry of the fifth line by dividing exactly down the middle with a comma and beginning each hemistich with the same expression − 'And suddenly ... and suddenly ...' (line 11); 'Now ... now ...' − each followed by the same verb with a different prefix (line 13). Hardly less noticeable is the repetition of *letit* ('she flies') at the end of line 11 and the beginning of line 12, or the back-to-back use of the same noun in two different cases (*nozhkoy nozhku*) which brings the stanza almost to its end. Inevitably, of course, these parallels are awash with delicate sound effects as vowels and consonants form up in their repetitive patterns. Other vowels and consonants, not involved in the mechanical contrasts, also join in; *odnoy nogoy ... pukh ot ust ...* (picking up the 'u' sound of the twice-used *vdrug* (suddenly) in the previous line), the chiasmus of initial consonants, b, n, n, b, in the last line.

Not that the sounds are of primary importance here. The impact of these lines works upon the visual imagination. It derives from the setting up of an unusually intricate system of exactly balanced repetitions, rhythms, analogues and parallels. Equivalence and symmetry, expressed both in stasis and in movement, are what matter most. In this way Pushkin almost succeeds in translating one art form into another. The ballet has been set down on the page. The theatre and its atmosphere, the people present all over the building, the soaring curtain, the stage, the musicians, the corps de ballet and the prima ballerina have been gently squeezed together into the fifty-eight words of a single *Onegin* stanza. And the greatest surprise of all, when we stand back to reflect on this exquisite poetry, is that this stanza is not part of the main purpose of the story; it appears to be incidental and parenthetic. Its actual reason for being is twofold. It forms part of the digressive pattern, the apparently rambling series of general observations on life, love, literature and art which is such an endearing character-istic of the novel as a whole. Rather more subtly, it is set up as a measure of Eugene Onegin's absurd propensity for missing out on beauty and goodness. In the next stanza (one, XXI) we shall see him blunder into the theatre, arriving late, look around at everything but the stage and then yawn the house down out of boredom. If he had been missing out on any old pantomime, his sin of omission might have been mitigated. But he has neglected even to notice Istomina in all her loveliness, and that must be beyond forgiveness.

As it happens, the second stanza selected for close considera-tion makes the same point about our negligent hero. Fifteen stanzas later on in the same chapter (one, XXXV) he returns home in the early morning, having been at an all-night ball. He is half-asleep and therefore fails to notice all the lovely things which are brought by the poet to our attention. Once again he has the misfortune to ignore not a cold, drizzly morning the like of which we should all be glad to miss, but a lovely winter scene full of delight on every side.

> Что ж мой Онегин? Полусонный
> В постелю с бала едет он;
> А Петербург неугомонный
> Уж барабаном пробужден.
> Встает купец, идет разносчик,
> На биржу тянется извозчик,
> С кувшином охтенка спешит,
> Под ней снег утренний хрустит,
> Проснулся утра шум приятный,
> Открыты ставни, трубный дым
> Столбом восходит голубым,
> И хлебник, немец аккуратный,
> В бумажном колпаке, не раз
> Уж отворял свой *васисдас*.

And Eugene? Half-awake, half-drowsing,
From ball to bed behold him come;
While Petersburg's already rousing,
Untirable, at sound of drum.
The merchant's up, the cabman's walking
Towards his stall, the pedlar's hawking;
See with their jugs the milk-girls go
And crisply crunch the morning snow.
The city's early sounds awake her;
Shutters are opened and the soft
Blue smoke of chimneys goes aloft,
And more than once the German baker,
Punctilious in his cotton cap,
Has opened up his serving trap.

Here we have another example of Pushkin's eye for charming realistic detail and his capacity for telling a much larger story than first meets the eye by miniaturisation and implication. The attentive reader ends up with far more information about the morning, the city, its people and the hero of the story than would seem possible in such a short space. As Onegin returns home to go to bed and sleep, the city of St Petersburg is doing the opposite, awakening to a new day. We observe a few of the citizens going about their early business – traders, stall-holders, carriage-drivers, a girl with a jug, a German baker. They are going out, getting started, opening up. The picture is wholly positive. They go willingly to work and the city and the morning welcome them. In the entire stanza (apart from the out-of-touch Eugene) there is not a single sour taste. Only one character shows any kind of reluctance and in his case it is understandable. He is the cab-driver, whose step is slow; he is used to having wheels beneath him. Everyone else seems to want the day to get under way because it holds promise. It makes a most agreeable scene, appealing as much to the ear as to the eye. Not only do we *see* these good, busy people, but we can also hear the beat of a loud, distant drum, the crunch of snow underfoot and the background city noise still subdued and gentle enough to be described as *priyatnyy*, 'pleasant'. We know from various clues that is is a delightfully clear, cold morning; visibility is good, chimney smoke rises straight up in a light-blue column into the morning air. This is Pushkin at his most genial. He gives us a picture so infectiously beautiful that you and I (though not, of course, Eugene) would want to get up early next day and see it for ourselves.

If laconic expressiveness is this poet's hallmark, nowhere will you find a better example of it than in this stanza, which also consists of fifty-eight words. These are doled out in very small portions – a couple for the merchant, four for the carriage-driver, nine for the girl from Okhta, and so on. Yet much information is imparted. With the slenderest of resources Pushkin produces an eloquently impressionistic vision of the city and hints at an important relationship between it and the hero.

The two half-identified citizens are of particular interest. This novel is full of unobtrusive little characters who flit rapidly in and out of the story. They are more important than they seem to be. Pushkin treats them with a warm, welcoming humour. This is his attitude to humanity at large; it is a major form of compensation for all the jaundiced nastiness which Onegin brings into the story and it certainly marks the real difference between the two men. Onegin would not so much as notice that such insignificant people exist; Pushkin sees them, cares about them and wishes them well. The funeral visitors in chapter one, neighbours and friends of the Larins in chapter two, a countryman driving out in the snow at the beginning of chapter five, the little boy in the same scene playing with his sledge and his dog, his worried mother – these, and other such people, unimportant, once-on, quickly forgotten characters populate the hidden recesses of the novel and remind us of the goodness of ordinary life. They are anticipated and represented by the young girl and the baker in this stanza.

First, the girl with the jug of milk, the very incarnation of morning freshness. She exudes youthfulness, prettiness, innocence and good purpose; she *would* be worth getting up early to watch. She is hurrying, perhaps because it is cold, perhaps just because she is young and young people do hurry. Why does she seem so charming? The answer lies probably in the name which she bears. She is an 'Okhtenka' (stress on the first syllable), which simply means that she comes from the district of Okhta in the eastern part of the city. This winsome word sounds like a pretty diminutive, though it is not. It was clearly selected by the poet *because* it sounds so sweet. Having chosen it, he took good care to follow up the possibilities; in the next line all four of the consonants in this word (kh, t, n, k) recur, and to good effect, in the imitation of morning show crunching underfoot. By simply sounding so nice she persuades us of her all-round attractiveness. Are there any lines in the whole poem lovelier than these?

С кувшином охтенка спешит,
Под ней снег утренний хрустит.

What we must not forget is that this girl is presented to us in those nine words alone.

Then the German baker, another charming early riser. He is a slightly comic figure, though endearingly portrayed and given a generous allocation of words over three whole lines. His character is that of the stereotyped German, meticulous; his demeanour is that of the traditional baker in his tall, white cotton cap. His Germanic origin hints at the cosmopolitanism of all capital cities but perhaps especially that of St Petersburg, which was created artificially not much more than a century before and which simply imported all the good things it needed, and all the specialists, from Italian architects to, as we now see, German tradesmen. The naming of his little window, his *vasisdas* ('Was ist das?') is an amusing touch; it provides the opportunity for one of the most attractive rhymes in the whole novel (a macaronic one with *ne raz*, 'more than once'). The fact that even at this early hour this window has been opened several times informs us of the industrious habits not only of the baker but of many another working-class St Petersburger. Like that of the Okhtenka, this miniature picture tells more than first meets the eye.

This good humoured stanza serves several purposes. It is relevant, realistic and simply part of the story. The opening rhetorical question is Pushkin's easy way of wrenching his narrative back on to the lines after a lengthy digression. The rest of it fills in the background pleasantly enough as Eugene makes his way home. It might also be described as a democratic stanza. Simply to notice and depict at some length such ordinary people going about such ordinary business, and to do so with fellow feeling rather than condescension, is still new to Russian literature. Pushkin does it all so spontaneously, with such gentleness, good humour and evident affection that he communicates more strongly than anything else a sense of deep sympathy with these unprivileged townsfolk. He likes them. He almost envies what Thomas Gray, speaking of their rural counterparts, had already described as 'their useful toil' and 'their destiny obscure'. Like Gray, Pushkin himself adds significantly to 'the short and simple annals of the poor'.

Unusual acoustic properties haunt the stanza. Even those that are obvious are so appropriate that they cannot fail to please the ear. The crunching Okhtenka is a case in point; another concerns the sound of the morning drum. Luckily the Russian word for drum is already onomatopoeic and quite long, so *baraban* is quickly pressed into service. It finds support in the following word *probuzhden* (awakened) and, more importantly, it was strongly anticipated one line earlier in the vigorous name of the city itself, *Peterburg*. A voiced plosive is a powerful consonant; four of them in two lines create all the energy needed for a good resonant drumming sound:

А Петербург неугомонный
Уж барабаном пробужден.

But those very lines contain another insistent, though less assertive sound. The vowel 'u' (much rounder and darker in Russian, as in the English word b<u>oo</u>m) appears four times, one of them stressed and another at the beginning of the line, virtually half-stressed. Alone, this series might be of small consequence, but in fact it fits into a broader pattern of no little importance. We shall soon see that this vowel becomes the most important one in the stanza, romping away with lines 8 and 9 where it rings out in five successive words, four of them stressed (*... utrennyy khrustit. Prosnulsya utra shum...*). The last two words, *utra shum*, actually mean 'the noise of morning' and it is with that low, booming vowel that the morning noise is associated. When we look closely we can see something unusual about this vowel; it appears all over the stanza. In fact, although it is not the most commonly encountered of the Russian vowels, here it makes no fewer than nineteen appearances, stressed or unstressed and once in its softer form 'yu.' Indeed, *it comes into every line.* Anyone who thinks that this does not seem all that remarkable should face the challenge of finding any other stanza in *Eugene Onegin* of which the same may be said. There is certainly not one in the first chapter. Thus the pleasant noise of morning hums in the background throughout the entire stanza, brought once to noticeable prominence and drowned out only once by the more insistent sound of the drum. The subtlety of the two lines quoted may now be fully sensed; they are doubly onomatopoeic. It is hardly surprising that they ring so true, sound so good and linger in the memory.

We have looked closely at two stanzas from the first chapter of *Eugene Onegin*. Neither is of great importance for the action. Both are beautiful, likely to catch the passing eye and please it. But it is not until you get right inside such creations and expose the skilful workmanship that some realisation may be gained of the quality of Pushkin's poetry. Several conclusions may be drawn from what we have seen. The artistry displayed is of the highest order, with expert manipulation of the chosen technical resources. There is an easy, almost casual air about the way Pushkin tells his story; he has such a natural manner with verses that they flow without constraint and appear to be near to normal, unpoetic, Russian. We shall soon see that this lightness of touch actually disguises not only perfect mastery of technique but also the existence in his work of solid content and serious ideas. There has been more misjudgement and underestimation of this area of Pushkin's achievement than anywhere else. Above all there is a greater density to Pushkin's stanzas than meets the unpractised eye. In these short paragraphs he implies much more than he states, reaching wide and probing deeply, filling out the background, creating atmosphere and often departing from cold objectivity to provide, or imply, a particular attitude to what is under description. All of this will determine the tone of what will turn out to be a great novel. We have glanced into the depths of two appealing but apparently inconsequential stanzas. They have turned out to be more richly rewarding than might have been anticipated. There are three hundred and sixty-four more waiting to be enjoyed.

Chapter 2

Shades of unreality

Simplicity seems to be the hallmark of *Eugene Onegin*. 'Tatyana falls in love with Onegin and nothing comes of it. Then he falls in love with her and nothing comes of it. End of novel.' So speaks one critic (Bayley: Introduction to the Charles Johnston translation, p. 15). If this were the full story there would be no case for considering *Eugene Onegin* to be a serious poem let alone a great novel. Of course it is not. This is anything but a straightforward narrative. The characters, their actions, their motivation, the ideas which they stir into circulation – all of these are elusive. Apparent simplicity proves to be illusory; the novel is difficult to interpret properly and impossible to pin down. Over the decades *Onegin* criticism has become increasingly complex and contradictory. All too often, without proper justification, explanation slides steadily into convoluted argument.

Let us put it plainly. Ever since its first appearance this novel has been subjected to distortion and misunderstanding. Warning signs have been ignored, partiality has been allowed a free hand and over-complication has fed upon itself. To a limited extent this is a good thing; a serious work of art must be capable of generating much discussion. Nor can all the complexities be resolved suddenly by a burst of new thinking. However, it will be useful to take account of some mistakes and contradictions which have arisen in this field. The ground must be cleared (yet again) before any new observations can be added to the discussion.

First, the difficulties. These cannot be overstated. More veils and shades, of disguise and concealment, have been cast over *Eugene Onegin* than any novel you are likely to encounter before the twentieth century. They need to be taken away, where possible, or penetrated with great care where that is the best that can be done. The first duty of every reader is to become aware of them and afterwards never forget their existence.

The story

The basic story-line of the novel runs as follows. Eugene Onegin was born in (or around) 1796. After a rather superficial education he emerged into St Petersburg society in 1812 and spent eight years in idleness and dissipation. When his uncle died, in 1820, leaving him a comfortable country estate, Onegin went to live there, only to find himself as bored with rural life as he had been in the city. (All of this is recounted in chapter one). He meets and apparently befriends a young neighbour, Lensky, who is in love with a local girl, Olga Larina (chapter two). Olga's sister, Tatyana, falls in love with Onegin and naively offers herself to him in a long letter (chapter three). Uninterested, Onegin rejects her approach and lives on in the country like a recluse. Months later Onegin is invited to Tatyana's name-day celebrations. By this time Lensky and Olga are planning their wedding (chapter four). Tatyana begins her name-day with a lurid nightmare in which she is chased by a bear, intimidated by monsters and rescued by Onegin, who then stabs Lensky. At the grand evening ball Onegin, angry with Lensky who had led him to expect a modest family occasion, monopolises Olga to an insulting degree. Lensky has no option but to challenge Onegin to a duel (chapter five). He is shot dead. Within half a year Olga has married a hussar and departed (chapter six). Onegin leaves the area. Tatyana visits his manor, browses through his books and realises what an insubstantial character he is. Her family then takes off to Moscow (chapter seven). About three years later Onegin arrives in St Petersburg where he meets Tatyana, now married to a prince and a prominent member of high society. In a letter he declares his love for her but she refuses him, saying that she will not betray her husband (chapter eight). The story concludes in the spring of 1825.

The presence of Pushkin

Pushkin himself creates an obvious problem. His presence in the novel is a major factor to be reckoned with; perhaps it goes even deeper than has been generally acknowledged. He tells the story and also, from time to time, takes part in it. His own preferences and dislikes are bound to lead us away from narrative objectivity. Sometimes he even apologises for doing things his way rather than according to normal standards. A good example arises at the beginning of chapter five in the description of winter. In one of the loveliest of all his passages (five, I and II) he gives us an impressionistic picture of what Tatyana sees as she looks out through the window on the first snowy morning in January 1821. The white yard, the flower-beds, roofs, fence, patterns on the window-panes, trees silvered over, jolly magpies, a peasant on his sledge, his horse snuffling at the snow, a passing wagon with its driver sitting, well wrapped up, on high, a peasant lad running his own little sledge along with his dog as a passenger and himself doing the horse-work, while his mother admonishes him through the window. This wonderful catalogue of objects, animals, people and activities presents a colourful and moving depiction of early winter. Its brevity, precision and its un-selective naturalness give it the ring of truth and beauty. Pushkin knows this, of course, and drives home his success by playing a little game with us. He apologises in the next stanza (III) for his lack of refinement in describing such ordinary sights; it is all nature and no elegance. Another poet, he says, would have done it much better, with soaring eloquence and more detail. He uses a footnote to turn our attention to just such a writer; 'See Vyazemsky's *First Snow*'. Anyone who turns to that poem will soon see what he means; eloquence and detail are there in abundance. Rhyming iambic hexameters (with a severe mid-line caesura and draconian end-stopping) by the yard; no fewer than one hundred and five lines, more than thirteen hundred soaring syllables given to scenic description and suitable philosophical thoughts, all of it culminating in this resonant apostrophe:

O first-born child of resplendent, sullen winter!
First snow, virginal fabric of our fields!

This is great literary fun. Having seen Pushkin at his best, we have then redoubled our pleasure through comparison with mediocrity. It does not matter that the confident poet has shown off a little. He has done so both on merit and with good humour based on an illusion of self-dismissiveness. What is significant is the way in which it all happened. Pushkin has manipulated everything, his own verses, the text of his novel, and us. There are not many novels in which this kind of thing occurs. The Russian poet has clearly learned a good deal from Laurence Sterne, whose toying with the reader in *Tristram Shandy* provided him with a model and a method.

But *Eugene Onegin* is not a comic novel. Playing with our expectations and sensibilities – which Pushkin continues to do throughout the novel – means something quite different when serious matters are in train. It means, for instance, that we never quite know where we are in relation to the truth. To take another example, when Onegin has finished his negative response to Tatyana, following receipt of an importunate letter from her, in comes the author with his own comment and a request for a sympathetic response from the reader too: 'You must agree, my reader, that our friend acted very nicely towards the sad Tatyana; not for the first time did he demonstrate real nobility of spirit ...' (four, XVIII). It is not at all clear what Pushkin is about. Is this a genuine endorsement of Eugene's conduct? Or is it the opposite, sarcasm intended to undermine the quality of his behaviour? In any case, why can't we be left to absorb the words and events, and then form our own conclusions? And this sort of thing is not uncommon. In the previous chapter Pushkin has asked similar things about Tatyana and her behaviour: 'Why is Tatyana, then, more guilty? Is it because, in her sweet simplicity, she does not know the meaning of deceit and she believes in her chosen dream? ...' (three, XXIV). The important point is that Pushkin is always there, in close proximity, directing our attention, joking with us, or pretending to do so, apparently underlining, but possibly subverting what has been said. There is nothing at all annoying about this. Quite the reverse: Pushkin is a kindly narrator, most of the time, and a genial companion. You warm to him and want more and more of him; he is so good at his job. The one certain thing, however, is that because of his unsecretive involvement in both the story and the text, you cannot rely on him for an impartial approach.

This uncertainty is of particular importance when it comes to assessing the main characters of the novel. Pushkin is a close friend of Onegin's and for Tatyana he entertains a quirky but admiring love. This kind of partiality distorts as it describes. Consider Onegin. Pushkin liked him as soon as they met because of Onegin's capacity for daydreaming, his inimitable strangeness and his sharp, cold wit (one, XLV). Even Pushkin had to overcome a sense of outrage at his vicious tongue, his bitter jokes and venomous epigrams, though these were something one could get used to (one, XLVI). It is interesting to note who changed whom. Pushkin did not mellow Onegin; it was Onegin who demanded and secured Pushkin's acquiescence before there could be any friendship. What kind of a basis is this for narrative trustworthiness? Pushkin is not just a friend, he is deeply involved with Onegin and, it would seem, slightly in awe of him. Their relationship certainly developed to the point where they were planning a long period of foreign travel together. The two men have much in common (though as the poet himself and many subsequent critics rightly point out, there are even stronger dissimilarities between them). Because of their closeness, an interesting question arises: when they were younger, could Pushkin not have done more to influence Onegin's awful character for the better? Could he not have indicated sometimes that his companion was going too far? It is not inconceivable that, even as he tells Onegin's story, Pushkin feels an oblique sense of responsibility for what happened, particularly for the death of Lensky. Does Pushkin perhaps take a share in Onegin's shortcomings and blameworthiness, either because he recognises too much of himself in his friend and hero, or because he knows he could have done more in advance to avert the apparently inevitable tragedy? These are not questions to which there are ready answers, but they are bound to arise when an author plays a part in his own novel. Above all, they deprive us of certainty. Pushkin introduces Onegin to us as *dobryy moy priyatel'*, 'my good friend', (*dobryy* also carrying connotations of kindness and niceness) and in the first chapter he refers at least eight times to his hero as 'my Onegin'. Every such reference entangles them further and leaves us with a growing sense that Pushkin cannot be immune from the effects of such closeness. We ought to suspect that his presentation of Onegin may be tendentious and apologetic. There is a serious possibility that the negative qualities of Eugene Onegin may have been underrepresented. With Tatyana the same thing occurs in reverse. Pushkin is so open about his love for this character that he is bound to see her, and to present her to us, in special colours. We shall have to face the possibility that behind the portrait of this charming young lady, as painted by the admiring author, hides a personality which others may have assessed as a shade less beguiling.

The other aspect of Pushkin's person which must give pause for thought is his sheer skill as a poet. There can be little doubt that our perception of events in this novel is greatly affected, and sometimes perhaps distorted by the beautiful manner of their presentation. The most obvious example concerns the death of Lensky. Pushkin's description of the duel (six, XXIX–XXXII) is so accomplished (as many critics, Nabokov foremost among them, have indicated), that the abiding impression gained from the whole incident is a positive one based on sheer admiration for the genius of the poet. This is all very well, but it has an unfortunate consequence: our sense of tragedy is dulled. In what purports to be the real world a lad of eighteen has been slaughtered with great cruelty two weeks before his wedding day; nothing should diminish our rage or impede the flow of our tears. Dulled also is our sense of blame. Onegin is surely beyond forgiveness for what he has done. But every reader who has studied this moving passage will find his emotions mixed rather than pure. Poor Lensky has been given short shrift and Onegin, if he has not exactly got away with it, somehow escapes the severest censure.

We must not imply that there is something wrong, or devious, or unpleasant in Pushkin's telling the story his way and parading his skills and knowledge as he does so. The reverse is true; the narrative tone of *Eugene Onegin* is a saving grace and a rare achievement. Pushkin purges his work as he goes, cleansing it from all kinds of excess – from Byronism, Romanticism, bookishness, seriousness, sentimentality. The whole text is bespattered with Pushkinisms: flashes of wit, displays of erudition, delicate irony and sniping sarcasm, humour darting into everything, refreshing touches of realism, all of which bring the narrator back time and again from the brink of intemperance. Not only does Pushkin continually adjust the narrative style, according to the passing need for humour, bathos, variety and so on, he even corrects his own adjustments. Thus he knows how to temper with light-heartedness his own tendency to ridicule; his reward is an ability to criticise and debunk without creating offence or committing any lapse of taste.

Consider the Romantic paraphernalia of *Eugene Onegin*: castles in the country, ill-starred lovers, moonlit nights, grave-yards, a nightmare with monsters and other apparitions, bouts of meditative melancholia, a dramatic duel and death, and the rest. All of this is decanted into acceptable realism by the immaculate taste and timing of a brilliantly endowed narrator. In order to appreciate the remarkable success of this novel in constricting its Romantic material, we need to consider what the story would be like if there were no Pushkin in it. This is not an exercise in abstraction. There exists a work composed entirely of *Eugene Onegin* with some of Pushkin's poetry but none of his narrative quality. This is, of course, Tchaikovsky's musical version, described by Nabokov as a 'silly opera' (vol. 2, p. 333) and by a more objective commentator as 'lush, dreamily sentimental romanticism' (Schmidgall, *Literature as Opera*, p. 219). Reading these words we realise precisely what the original novel has avoided and what a debt of gratitude we owe to our puckish narrator.

Pushkin's style is, then, his greatest attribute. But this very quality must be said to impede understanding. We have seen several examples of ways in which the story, the events and the characters of *Eugene Onegin* are inevitably distorted by the narrator and his great talent. Even though there is no possibility of applying any kind of accurate corrective to our reading so that we stay always as near to the truth as possible, at least we should be aware of the indeterminacy of much that is being purveyed. This novel, so different in style from its prose confrères in the nineteenth century, needs to be read and recalled with great caution. With this warning in mind we shall be less likely to jump to false conclusions when reflecting on the novel as a whole.

Inherited perceptions of *Eugene Onegin*

Much has been written about this novel. Many critics grinding many axes have made it their own. It has been twisted into all sorts of different shapes; apparently anyone can do what he likes with it. Few novels have become so encrusted with well-meaning efforts at interpretation. In order to achieve full understanding the reader must subject these inherited opinions to the closest scrutiny and refuse to be persuaded in advance by what the loudest voices have proclaimed.

One characteristic above all strikes the reader of *Onegin* criticism; it is contradictory. Every twenty years or so since the novel first appeared a critical article has seemed to establish a new line of thinking about it. Not infrequently this has involved a complete about-face. Thus, Vissarion Belinsky claims in 1844 that Eugene Onegin is 'simply a nice fellow', 'his nature was very fine'; the blame for his misconduct belongs to the age and the society in which he lived. (This means unreformed, unmodernised Russia drifting towards its age of greatest oppression under Nicholas I). Belinsky holds that the very purpose of the novel is to criticise the shortcomings of contemporary society, by depicting a man of great potential who can find no means of realising it because of his stifling surroundings. Scarcely two decades had passed when Dmitri

Pisarev claimed the opposite: '*Eugene Onegin* is nothing more than a vivid and glittering apotheosis of the dreary and senseless *status quo.*' Twenty years on (1880), no less a personage than Fyodor Dostoyevsky appropriates the novel for himself and for Russia: *Eugene Onegin* is about Russia's destiny and Eugene himself should be seen as an estranged figure with no faith in his motherland, an object lesson in patriotic inadequacy. By the end of the century (1897) Dmitri Merezhkovsky puts the case the other way round: the novel is not Russian but a work of universal genius and, as for the hero, he should be seen as a self-willed egoist, a man distinguished from common humanity and a positive force. Into the twentieth century, and attitudes change again. Now we are led to believe that the real achievement of this unusual work lies less in the realm of characters and ideas than in its very clever form and style. And all the time people have argued about the question of realism, some believing that this is its greatest asset, others asserting that it is not realistic at all but a complex amalgam of literary allusions and cultural echoes, a grand and virtuoso display of parody.

The general impression created by this great corpus of critical ideas seems to be that *Eugene Onegin* is an impenetrably complex work which will yield its secrets only to learned minds. In fact, the opposite is true; in itself it is a delightful work, simply told and readily understandable. The trouble is that the inherited critical traditions are so powerful that they continue to influence modern thinking. Some ideas which ought to have been dismissed by now, continue to enjoy currency. A good example may be seen in the Belinskian tradition. A modern version of this, popular in Soviet Russia, has taken up what was only the ghost of an idea in the author's mind − that Onegin might eventually have become a Decembrist (a member of the group standing for constitutional reform which mounted a disastrously unsuccessful uprising in December 1825). The western variation on this theme ignores Decembrism but still sees the hero of the novel, not as a dangerous man responsible for his own misdeeds, but as a suffering individual caught up in the national crisis. These are the same old-fashioned thoughts which continue to be applied also to Mikhail Lermontov's novel, *A Hero of Our Time*. A recent critic linked these two authors in a reference to *Sashka*, a poem by Lermontov written in *Onegin* stanzas; Lermontov is to be congratulated because he 'catches the essentials of Pushkin's masterpiece, in that his hero is shown as *the predictable product of his environment*' (Brown, *History of Russian Literature*, p. 83, italics added). When commentators move away from this essentially political interpretation of the novel they sometimes nevertheless continue to work within the tradition initiated by Belinsky. It is not uncommon, for instance, for them to stress the extent to which Onegin was trapped by contemporary convention rather than free to operate as an individual. Sometimes even the hoary old hand of fate is invoked, the implication being that the actions of the main characters were predetermined by some malign force of destiny. In this way a generally defensive and apologetic attitude has grown up around Eugene Onegin in particular. From whatever angle you consider his behaviour, allowances have to be made; external forces of one kind or another made it impossibly difficult for him to act differently from the way he did. Thus he is not wholly to blame even for the misdeeds which he perpetrated.

It is time to shrug off this protective covering and compel Onegin to stand up for his own actions, undefended by tendentious theory. Even if he is to some extent a child of his time, and for that matter a member of a strong European literary tradition — that of the alienated Romantic — this hero offers greater interest when taken out of his historical context. He needs to be examined primarily in terms of his psychology and moral responsibility. If we can bring this about we shall enhance the standing of Pushkin's novel by relating it to universal rather than temporary historical truth. For the moment it is sufficient to take account of the voluminous *Onegin* criticism which, for all its exegetic brilliance, stands in danger of dazzling and puzzling the new reader of this novel. It is not to be ignored on any account, but we must look with some scepticism even on some of its most confident assertions and refuse to surrender to any of its apparently established precepts.

Morning into midnight

Another unusual characteristic of *Eugene Onegin* is that it is bathed in a peculiar light. It is predominantly a nocturnal novel. Almost all the vital developments take place during the hours of darkness (though they tend to be resolved in the cold light of day) and most of the set-piece scenes of the novel will be recalled as occurring under artificial light or by moonlight. Its atmosphere is determined mainly be coloured brilliance or a half-lit glow. References to the sun and moon abound, at the rate of five to one in favour of the moon. We seem to be moving most of the time in a world that is artificial and unreal. The strange illumination of *Eugene Onegin* is a mystifying force that we must reckon with.

By day we watch Onegin travelling (chapter one), suffering boredom in the country and getting to know Lensky (chapter two). We also observe Olga and Lensky in love (chapters two and four), the first part of Tatyana's name-day celebrations (chapter five) and, much later, Tatyana travelling with the family to Moscow (chapter seven). All of this is essentially background material; it just happens to take place in the day-time and is reported as doing so. Three other events occurring by day are of great significance both in themselves and particularly as *daytime events*: the all-important duel (chapter six), Tatyana's second visit to Onegin's castle (chapter seven), and her final showdown with Onegin (chapter eight). We shall have more to say of them.

The evening and night-time events are, without exception, important ones. These include virtually the whole of Onegin's activity in the city (chapter one); Tatyana's double declaration of love, first to her nurse and then in the famous letter to Onegin (chapter three); his rejection of her, which takes place out of doors, but after sunset when the evening samovar is in full play (chapter four); Tatyana's protracted nightmare (which takes place at night and also describes night-time activities) and the important part of the name-day celebrations, the winter evening ball (chapter five); Tatyana's first visit to Onegin's castle and her first meeting with her future husband (chapter seven), as well as her surprising reunion with Onegin early in chapter eight.

The first principle which we can see at work here is that of alternation. Chapters which place the emphasis on night-time activities (one, three and five) are succeeded by predominantly daytime ones (two, four and six). This amounts to a satisfying stylistic device, a further enhancement of the acknowledged sense of structure and rhythm which underlies the story. The last two chapters have important events by night and by day. Chapter seven begins and ends by night; the final chapter begins by night and ends during the daytime.

The characters are grouped according to their affinities for daylight or darkness. Both Pushkin and Lensky are daytime creatures. Pushkin certainly used to like the evening and night, as we learn from his recollections of late hours spent with Onegin (one, XLV–XLVII), but he is equally adjusted to the daylight, apparently preferring it as time goes by. Many are the occasions when he describes lovingly a daytime scene which Onegin would either have failed to notice or would have positively disliked. One of the ways in which Pushkin draws a clear distinction between himself and Onegin is to point out (one, LV–LVI) that, whereas Onegin was always bored by the countryside, he himself loved to get up in the morning with a sense of liberation, walk down by the lake and revel in the pleasures of nature. In this respect Pushkin is behaving like a normal person; now and again he enjoys the evening and the night but his natural element is that of the day. Lensky is rather similar. After falling in love, it is true, he can see the traditional charms of moonlight and night-time (two, XXII; four, XXV), but he is really a creature of the day along with his Olga, who is herself described as 'Always as merry as the morning' (two, XXIII). There is no emphasis whatever on their love of darkness. In their innocent naiveté they are content to spend their daylight hours together reading to each other, playing chess and letting others see their happy love.

The one chapter (six) which is dominated by Lensky, and which brings him to his death, is acted out in the early light of a sunny day. He, too, is someone who can take darkness but prefers the day.

Onegin and Tatyana are not like this. They both abhor daytime. They cannot thrive, and they seem hardly to exist, before the hours of darkness, when suddenly they come to life. Onegin takes refuge in glittering, artificial light, whereas Tatyana cleaves to the darkness for its own sake, but they are as one in retreating from daylight. The inverted pattern of Onegin's existence in St Petersburg is such that he is said to be 'turning morning into midnight' (one, XXXVI). Although he has to endure a small part of the daylight hours, he does so strolling indifferently on the boulevard. His excitement, real if short-lived, is sensed only when the evening begins.

> Now it is dark: he gets into a sledge.
> "Come on, get going!" is the cry ...   (one, XVI)

We know from the narrative that this journey takes him first to dinner with a friend, then to the theatre and, later still, to a ball from which he returns in the early morning. Throughout the hours of darkness he is fully occupied. We also know that this is his regular routine.

> He will wake up in the afternoon, and once again
> His life is prepared for him until next morning,
> Monotonous and motley,
> And tomorrow the same as yesterday.   (one, XXXVI)

Although he makes attempts to break out of this cycle, he succeeds only in making matters worse. Abandoning the pleasures of the flesh for the life of the mind, he proves incapable of concentrating on either writing or reading (one, XLIII–XLIV). Later on (one, LIII–LIV) he will decline into lassitude after only two days in the countryside, and fail to rise again on the third. In the dark hours he was never happy, but he remained always active, finding some temporary excitement and entertainment. In the daytime he can find nothing at all to do. In fact the whole tragedy of Lensky stems from the inability of Onegin to occupy himself during the empty day. Their false friendship, with its grisly outcome, was founded on the nothingness that resulted from this deficiency. As the poet says,

> In this way people (I'm the first to admit)
> Become friends *from having nothing to do*.   (two, XIII)
>   (Pushkin's italics)

Tatyana must be regarded as suffering from the same condition but in a more extreme form; she is a devotee of darkness itself. Ironically, this is indicated perhaps most clearly in the only reference in the novel which links her to the *sun*. Early in chapter five (five, IV) we are told of Tatyana's love of the Russian winter. The poet-narrator informs us − in a single line − that she does like the sunlight when it is reflected in hoar-frost, but he adds hastily, and at greater length (over the next five lines), that her preference is for the pink snow during the twilight hours and even more for the darkness of freezing evenings. All of this is a prelude to a recitation of her belief in omens, her fortune-telling, her attempt to guess her bridegroom's name out of doors on a frosty night, and then the entire sequence of her nightmare. This is the longest run of stanzas devoted exclusively to the dark in the whole novel. There are seventeen of them (five, V−XXI). The single reference to the sun, an oblique one at that, is engulfed by darkness within its own stanza and utterly eliminated from the memory by all that follows. Tatyana's obsession with the dark hours could hardly be better expressed. Nor could the contrast between the two sisters. When Tatyana awakens at last, her first perceptions are of the crimson dawn and Olga, an obvious creature of the daylight, who is appropriately described as 'rosier than the Northern Aurora and lighter than a swallow' (five, XXI).

The one reference which links Tatyana to the sun can only have been set up for demolition. Tatyana has no kinship whatsoever with that heavenly body. Her dealings are with the moon. In this novel it virtually belongs to her and there are times when she almost depends upon it for companionship, encouragement or inspiration. Consider the famous and beautiful scene in which Tatyana first articulates her love for Onegin and then writes to him (three, XVI–XXI). The moon is so strong a participant in these events that it seems to have a determining, rather than merely decorative, presence. The word *luna* is used five times in the space of three of these stanzas (XVI, XX and XXI). Its first appearance is wonderfully reassuring. Pushkin has been busy warning us directly that Tatyana is heading for destruction: 'I weep tears along with you ... You shall perish, my dear girl ...' (three, XV). Tatyana now walks out into the garden, about to face her destiny. What she needs most of all is a familiar, protective spirit to sustain her. It is there in the warm night and particularly the moonlight:

> Night comes on; the moon goes round
> Patrolling the distant vault of heaven.   (three, XVI)

Tatyana's old companion, the moon, is not just there to meet her: the word *dozorom*, 'on patrol', with its connotations of dependability and watchfulness, links itself to the phrase 'vault of heaven', raising the status of the moon virtually to that of guardian angel. The vulnerable heroine has her protectress. Renewed reassurance keeps coming from the same quarter. Having breathed out the words, 'I am in love ...' three times, Tatyana must be slightly shocked at her own audacity. But she feels confident enough to dismiss her nurse and no wonder. The guardian angel is still at hand.

> And meantime the moon shone
> And with a dark light irradiated
> Tatyana's pale charms ...   (three, XX)

Protection now turns into something even more valuable – inspiration. We do not have to guess from the circumstances that this is so; Pushkin tells us directly. That same stanza ends with a remarkable piece of poetry. In order to ensure that the dangerously high-flying sentiments are kept within bounds the poet diverts our attention to the grey-haired old nurse, and specifically to what she is wearing, something that we should now call a long body-warmer. This prosaic detail is important. Insulated by it from any sense of emotional excess, Pushkin is able to let the visual span, and with it the imagination, soar to the heavens once again. There, unsurprisingly, the moon is still waiting for Tatyana, but this time she is actually described as 'inspirational'. This is useful information, which we need for a full understanding of Tatyana but, as it happens, the Russian word is in itself an inspired one, because it has been such a delicious sound, *vdokhnovitel'noy*. One of Pushkin's most delightful terminal couplets breathes out the stillness and beauty of the night and, at the same time, reminds us of the all-important role that the moon is playing for the heroine:

> And in the stillness everything slumbered
> In the light of the inspirational moon. (three, XX)

There is more. Tatyana needs to draw even greater strength from her guardian. She does so immediately, at the start of the next stanza:

> And Tatyana's heart was ranging far away,
> As she looked at the moon. (three, XXI)

The possibility of writing to Onegin occurs to her at this very moment, ('Suddenly an idea was born in her mind'); it seems almost to have come from the moon herself. The nurse is instantly dismissed and Tatyana begins to write. Before she does so, still further reassurance comes from above:

> ... And now here she is alone.
> All is still. The moon gives her light. (three, XXI)

The last expression, 'The moon gives her light', is borrowed from Vladimir Nabokov's translation, which puts it well. The Russian version, lacking the verb 'give', is slightly odd, literally meaning 'The moon shines to her'. The unexpected dative case, 'to her', suggests a new kind of intimate relationship between her and the giver of the light. In any case, what matters here is the ultimate confirmation for the heroine that she is doing the right thing and need not worry. She has taken her guidance from the highest authority available to the physical senses and all the signals are good. In this lovely passage there is a real impression that matters are taken out of Tatyana's hands; control is assumed by the supernatural forces in which this girl is so naturally interested. Only a couple of stanzas later Pushkin will tell us, by means of a rhetorical question, that Tatyana is 'endowed by the heavens with a restless imagination' (three, XXIV). This figurative assertion seems nearer to the literal truth than one might think. Finally, we cannot but notice that once the letter is written, which means in the very first stanza after its recitation, the moon goes off duty:

> But now at last the moonbeams
> Are losing their glow ...   (three, XXXII)

At least six compelling lunar references in the space of a few stanzas have told an interesting story. The very least they have done is to confirm Tatyana in the role of a dedicated person of the dark hours. This is neither the beginning nor the end of that story; there are at least a dozen more references linking Tatyana with the moon and also to the evening, the night, murkiness and darkness.

The three dominating personalities in *Eugene Onegin* are Alexander Pushkin, Eugene Onegin himself and Tatyana Larina. Pushkin makes a noticeable appearance in about ninety stanzas, about a quarter of the novel. Onegin has the lion's share, nearing one hundred and fifty stanzas, a good two fifths of them. Tatyana is not far behind; she takes exactly a third, just over one hundred and twenty stanzas. After the first chapter, which is devoted exclusively to Onegin (and Pushkin), Tatyana dominates the novel by a large margin; she has all her one hundred and twenty stanzas to come whereas Onegin has only about one hundred left. Onegin and Tatyana, appearing separately or together, occupy virtually two thirds of the entire text. Since both of them are night-time personalities, it is scarcely surprising that the overall atmosphere of the novel is predominantly nocturnal, with subdued or unnatural illumination prevailing, or that most of the serious activity occurs during the late hours. However, as we noted above, there are three particular scenes in the novel which do not fit this pattern; they involve the night-time characters, they are of critical importance in the story and they take place during the day. These are the duel (chapter six), Tatyana's return visit to Onegin's castle (chapter seven) and the final confrontation between hero and heroine (chapter eight). Each of these is a scene of resolution in which a particular issue is settled; each is preceded by the development of expectations built up earlier, after sunset.

The visit to the castle is the least significant of the three. It is true that Tatyana is paying a return visit, having gone there the night before accompanied and therefore encouraged by the moon (which is referred to specifically in seven, XV and XIX), and now she returns in the morning, apparently in the cold light of day. But there is no mention of clarity, let alone sunlight. Nevertheless, this is day following night, and Tatyana does come to some conclusions for which the sun's clear rays may claim some oblique responsibility. In particular, she learns for the first time that Eugene Onegin is a man of insubstantial character. She is not sure what he *is* exactly, but she can see that his personality is unreal and immaterial. Her concept of him is narrowed and reduced. This is a great step forward in her perception, and surely one which can never be retraced. It must not be forgotten (though it usually is) when her subsequent attitude to him, during their encounters in the last chapter, is under review.

The other two events take the same form – matters building up in the evening to be resolved later on in the daytime – but with greater clarity. At the end of chapter five, approaching supper time, in the unreal world of the ballroom, we witness the build-up of events which will lead to the duel. Onegin monopolizes Olga at the ball and flirts with her outrageously. The world depicted during the aftermath is anything but unreal. Lensky's second, Zaretsky, delivers the challenge to Onegin in the light of morning. Lensky himself that day watches the sun in a manner reminiscent of Tatyana's glancing over her shoulder at the moon: 'He kept consulting the sun as if it were a watch' (six, XIII). Next morning, although the duel was planned for a time before daybreak (XII), Onegin oversleeps.

('By now the sun is riding high ...' (XXIV)). The adversaries
have been overtaken by daylight. The sun stays with them
throughout and is used figuratively to represent the actual
moment of Lensky's collapse and death:

> Thus, slowly, down the mountain-side,
> Under the sparkling, resplendent sun,
> A great block of snow descends ...   (six, XXXI)

A similar pattern recurs in the final chapter. Onegin encounters Tatyana in that fateful place, the ballroom (eight,
XVII); their second meeting is at a soirée (XXI). Here, ostensibly
on his own ground, where illusions can be built up and sustained, he falls in love with her, but this issue is another which
can only be resolved in the real world, in daylight. He sets
out for his final encounter with Tatyana on a spring morning.
The omens could not be worse. The clarity and the beauty
of the day are brought out by Pushkin in a couple of lines
of real poetic quality:

> Несется вдоль Невы в санях.
> На синих, иссеченных льдах
> Играет солнце ...   (six, XXXIX)

> He speeds along the Neva in his sledge.
> On the blue blocks of chopped out ice
> The sun plays ...

That sun is his enemy. It betokens reality, and the truth is
that his proposed relationship with Tatyana, whatever it may
be, is not going to come about.

It may seem fanciful to draw attention in so much detail
to a single aspect of the story, and one which has not been
taken so seriously before, but there are good reasons for looking
at *Eugene Onegin* in this way. The difference between night
and day in this novel is not simply a matter of the characters'
personal preference for darkness over daylight. Close consideration of the character and attitudes of the main protagonists
will show that those who shun the day — which means the
hero and heroine — are foolishly guilty of running away from
the demands and necessities of real life. They cling to illusions

and build their lives on falsehood. It is well established in *Onegin* criticism that both Eugene and Tatyana have been singularly influenced by what they have read in European literature. We can see that their vicarious way of living, through close identification with fictional heroes and heroines such as Byron's Childe Harold, Richardson's Clarissa Harlowe, Rousseau's Julie d'Etanges and Mme de Staël's Delphine d'Albemar, amounts to a serious personality deficiency. This hero and heroine have lost all capacity for the living of a natural and ordinary life. Their first concern is a negative one — to run away from reality; in doing so they come to grief. The futility, stupidity and sheer danger of such behaviour may be somewhat clouded over by the sympathetic personality and the lovely poetry of Alexander Pushkin, but even he cannot hide the injunction arising so clearly from his own story. Face the truth, he tells us by oblique implication, and you will have a better chance of forming proper relationships, as well as building a good and happy life, than those who are addicted to falsity and delusion. This is one of the most serious ideas in the novel and, because of its universal applicability, it deserves singular emphasis.

The second reason for peering closely at the strange illumination of *Eugene Onegin* is to avoid further misjudgement. It is not unreasonable to claim that all four leading characters in this story have suffered misinterpretation and need to be looked at more carefully. One of the reasons for this, particularly in the case of the hero and heroine, is that they have hidden in the shadows or reflected a false light. Their egregious abnormality has had its contours softened. Their shortcomings have been mitigated. This is to say that Eugene Onegin is actually more odious than many people have realised and Tatyana is possibly less enchanting. At the same time Lensky hardly deserves the condescension and mockery to which he has been treated. As for Olga, she should be relieved of some of the ridicule and blame which she has been made to carry. We must look at each of them in turn, and do so in the cold light of day.

Chapter 3

The unreal reputations of Eugene Onegin and Tatyana Larina

Eugene Onegin

Eugene Onegin is generally seen as a complex and rather mysterious figure; he is often described as an enigma. The explanations of his character are as varied as they are numerous. However, they do have one thing in common: a tendency to absolve Onegin from complete blame for his actions. Perhaps the mushrooming of explanations and the a priori willingness to mitigate Onegin's guilt are connected. Most critics start from the premise that there must be more to Onegin's awfulness than bad character alone. If we were to regard him at the outset as a mature man to be held fully responsible for all that he says and does, this simpler approach might cut through some of the complexities. This is what we shall now try to do.

Guilty or not guilty?

First, the question of his culpability and its mitigation. What is he guilty of, and what do people say about his blame-worthiness? He is to be arraigned for selfishness and anti-social behaviour of such an extreme kind that they do not balk at cruelty or even murder. Not content with insulting and humiliating most of the people he encountered, for no good reason beyond entertainment, Onegin eventually went so far as to shoot dead, wilfully and under avoidable circum-stances, a naive youth who stood on the brink of marriage to an attractive young country girl. The reasons which lie behind this vicious act, although not immediately obvious, are comprehensible and consistent. Thus we accuse him of appalling general behaviour and of one specific act of horrific violence. He is not just an annoying presence in society; he is a deadly danger.

This appears to be the truth of the matter, but it is not usual to hear it stated so directly. On the contrary, custom has it that excuses must be found to take some of the blame away from this young man, whatever he may have done. For instance, Vladimir Nabokov, the one person who might have claimed to know more about this novel than anyone else, says of Onegin's behaviour during the duel, 'He fires first and shoots to kill, which is quite out of character' (vol. 3, p. 41). A recent translator of *Eugene Onegin*, Walter Arndt, describes the hero as 'a helpless child of his age' (p. xvii). This accords with Richard Freeborn's description of him as 'beyond doubt a phenomenon of this time' (*Rise of the Russian Novel*, p. 23). John Bayley shows the duelling Onegin to be gripped by uncontrollable external powers when he speaks of 'the blank necessity which has suddenly taken over' (*Pushkin: A Comparative Study*, p. 257). J. Douglas Clayton, extrapolating from Yuri Lotman, explains that 'Onegin is an individual who is "locked into" codes of behaviour which make him behave like an automaton and which deprive him of the ability to express his free will and be a human being' (*Ice and Flame*, p. 150). W. M. Todd states that he 'lacks even the relative independence ... to place friendship above the more compelling conventions and seek a reconciliation [with Lensky]' (*Fiction and Society*, p. 133). Freeborn again: 'The despotism of social orthodoxy is as important as Fate ... in determining Onegin's character and ... behaviour' (*Rise of the Russian Novel*, p. 25). Arndt again: 'Not so much Tsarist repression as the ubiquitous literary *mal du siècle* might be made responsible for Onegin's failure, (*Eugene Onegin*, pp. xvii–xviii). Against this we can set the following broad explanation published as recently as 1986 by W. E. Brown: 'Onegin ... is actually determined by [contemporary Russian] society *in all his actions*' (italics supplied) (*History of Russian Literature*, p. 78).

This is powerful advocacy. Onegin has friends in the right places, determined to get him off. Unfortunately they are united only in this determination. All agree that he cannot be asked to bear the full weight of blame. The various pleas in mitigation, based on Fate, Tsarist oppression, *mal du siècle* or whatever else, may conceivably explain part of the problem presented by this character, but no one of them is better than any other. The trouble is that they deal with the circumstances surrounding Eugene Onegin rather than with the man himself and his psychology. The same circumstances, incidentally, surrounded all the other young men of the day, the ones who did not become misfits and murderers.

Imaginary superiority

Here we run into a further difficulty. There have been other advocates still who claim that, in acting as he did in this novel, Onegin sets himself apart from his feeble contemporaries in some *positive* kind of way. Guiltiest of all in this respect is no less a figure than the author himself who, at the beginning of the final chapter, anticipates our judgemental attitude towards Onegin and objects to it in terms which tell us more about his own partiality than about Onegin's possible innocence: 'Then why do you report on him so unfavourably? Is it because we go on and on passing judgement about everything? Because smug nonentity either berates or derides the rash behaviour of ardent spirits? Because wit, loving spaciousness, cramps everything? Because all too often we are glad to take words for deeds? Because stupidity is volatile and evil? Because trifling nonsense is important to important people, and because the only thing which fits us well and doesn't seem strange is mediocrity?' (eight, IX). This strange outburst, negated elsewhere in outright condemnation by Pushkin of his hero's behaviour, contains ideas which have actually been taken up by responsible people. Belinsky, Dostoyevsky and Merezhkovsky have all supported the belief that Onegin is really a thwarted idealist with energies which set him, at least potentially, *above* the rest of his contemporaries. It is in my view a despicable stance to adopt, baseless and misleading. Eugene Onegin's insubstantial character is such that he cannot deal with the ordinary problems of everyday life. There is no evidence anywhere to suggest that he is really a man of great strength. If ever he stands out from those around him it is for the most superficial and unpleasant of reasons − he does possess a quick intelligence and a mordant wit, which he puts always to destructive use. When the conversation gets at all serious, he retreats into a knowing silence intended to suggest expertise which he does not have. In this context the epigraph to the whole novel is both accurate and instructive. Translated from the French, it says, 'Steeped in vanity, he possessed even more of that kind of pride which acknowledges good and bad actions with equal indifference, owing to a sense of superiority which is perhaps imaginary.' Pushkin himself, having first toyed with the phrase 'superiority over other people', replaced this with the assertion that any such superiority exists only in the imagination. That is the best place to leave it.

The question of his blameworthiness is worth pursuing more closely. Even assuming that there is some truth in the idea that Onegin's actions were dictated not by his own will but by outside circumstances, it is surely a reductive step to think of the novel in these terms. If the main thrust of the story really was directed against Tsarist oppressiveness it would be a smaller achievement, of interest primarily to political historians. We shall hope to do better than this, by proposing that Pushkin is really dealing with issues of broader significance to humanity at large, questions of human psychology and moral responsibility.

The Byronic background

Perhaps the first strand to be disentangled is the literary one. It is clear that the literary antecedents of *Eugene Onegin* must be taken seriously. Pushkin draws on writers as disparate as Shakespeare, Sterne and Byron; Tatyana is partly formed by her reading of epistolary novels by Richardson, Rousseau and Mme de Staël. What about Onegin? Despite associations with Werther, Adolphe, René and other male heroes, he is most readily compared with those of Byron, that is Don Juan and particularly Childe Harold. Pushkin is so conscious of the spirit of Byron that he feels a need to dissociate himself (especially in chapter one, LVI). Onegin is linked specifically with Childe Harold early and late in the novel (one, XXXVIII and seven, XXIV). The best way to indicate the great void which separates the two is merely to glance at the way each is first introduced. Here is Byron:

> Whilome in Albion's isle there dwelt a youth ...
> Who ne in virtue's ways did take delight ...
> Ah me! in sooth he was a shameless wight ...
> Childe Harold was he hight ...   (Canto I, 2)

And here, by contrast, is Pushkin:

> With the hero of my novel,
> Here and now without introductions,
> Let me acquaint you:
> Onegin, a good friend of mine,
> Was born on the banks of the Neva,
> Where maybe you were born,
> My reader ...   (one, II)

To cope with Byron's language (rather than Pushkin's) you will need a dictionary. It is high-flown archaic English, exclamatory, rhetorical and − even allowing for parody − it is self-consciously poetic. (As such it is well suited to the stiff Spenserian stanza to which we referred in chapter one). The result is an abstract, other-worldly, scarcely credible, rather uninteresting hero. By contrast, Pushkin's language is normal, everyday Russian, colloquial, engaging, thoroughly unpoetic. Give or take a few slight inversions these are the very words that a speaker would use when performing an introduction. (The one archaic word, *bregakh* (banks), is lightly ironical, imparting a little extra grandeur in passing to the already splendid River Neva). The result is a credible, here-and-now protagonist, who seems like part of the real world known to Pushkin, you and me. He excites our interest and will sustain it. He continues to be read, delighting and infuriating each successive generation of Russian readers.

The 'Byronic hero' − a man of brooding melancholy, self-absorption, pride and cynical defiance, a figure of mystery, prematurely ageing – was well known to Pushkin. Onegin's attitude and behaviour may owe a good deal to Childe Harold and other such Romantic heroes, but his presentation does not. Nor is there any close association between them. It will be no use reading or re-reading Byron for real clues to Onegin's behaviour. It has the Byronic hero as its starting point but becomes interesting and significant only when developing further. A Childe Harold (or, for that matter, a Don Juan, a Werther, René or Adolphe) capable of murdering a young companion is unthinkable and the fascinating part of Onegin's personality will turn out to be precisely that area to which the Byronic hero has no access. For this reason we may step quickly over the issue of Onegin's antecedents in European literature. As to the *mal du siècle*, this is what Onegin began with; our interest must be focused upon how he ended up.

In and out of character

Careful examination of Eugene Onegin's career suggests a high degree of consistency, which scarcely redounds to his credit since he is consistently unpleasant and often nothing less than wicked. Anomalies there are, but not always where indicated by traditional *Onegin* criticism; the worst of these has less to do with Onegin's personality than with Pushkin's inability to sustain logical characterisation. Virtually everything we see Onegin do, including the rejection of Tatyana and the duel, seems to be broadly 'in character' right up to the last chapter. The only thing that is really difficult to take from this wrecked personality is the idea of his arid soul being affected so deeply by love for Tatyana in the closing scenes.

Onegin's character is determined, and almost at once lightly disguised, in the first few stanzas. We ought to draw serious conclusions from his opening interior monologue, but Pushkin persuades us not to do so. The acerbic tone of the first stanza is the true Onegin. He has no good word for the dying uncle who has left him a fortune. Apparently the only respectable thing the old man has ever done in his life is to have fallen seriously ill and that should be taken as a good example to everyone. We are not to know at this early juncture, but these sentiments, which tell us nothing about the uncle, speak volumes about Onegin and his unassailable misanthropy. The sixth, seventh and eighth lines of this opening stanza, and then the last two, display what looks like understandable impatience of a kind that anyone might experience, faced with the prospect of looking after an unloved invalid, but they do take frankness a shade too far:

> But, heavens above, what a bore
> To sit there with an invalid day and night
> And never move a step away ...
> To sigh and think to yourself,
> 'When *will* the devil take you off?'

Onegin scores well for honesty, even though the lines are spoken inwardly. He articulates what others, more squeamish, might feel but not express. Nevertheless his uncharitable ideas and emphatic tone leave a disagreeable impression. Like Pushkin (in one, XLVI) we too ought to find Onegin's language embarrassingly sharp-edged and difficult to get used to. And Pushkin, knowing his man in advance, chooses to present this unflattering image of the hero at the outset. The negative picture will be confirmed time and again in the ensuing pages, but for the time being the author is at pains to detract from it. If the poison of a bad impression is administered in this opening stanza, by the time we have read a few more an antidote will have been applied.

Onegin gains the sweetest of introductions in the next stanza (II), one of chattiness and geniality, in the midst of which the words 'my good (or kind) friend' begin to win us over to him. In the third stanza, we hear that in childhood our hero was seen as a boisterous but essentially nice lad. It is at this early point that an interesting idea is inserted. Onegin's cheery French tutor, we are told, 'taught him everything in a joking manner, did not weary him with moral strictures and gave him only a slight scolding for his naughtiness.' Could this be the hint of a proposal that any future depravity shown by the hero might be traceable to a deficient moral education when young? We must be on our guard. This circumstance, which might be taken as an explanation of his adult condition, must not be accepted as an excuse for it. Pushkin goes further. In the fourth stanza we learn that the society into which the young Onegin stepped in his late teens made few demands when judging a newcomer's mind and personality. All you needed to do was display the right clothes and hairstyle, speak and write fluent French, dance a passable mazurka and know how to bow politely. Pushkin's touch is light enough, but there can be no doubting the sarcasm of his remarks as he eases his hero into good society. This is not to say that Pushkin is on the point of *blaming* society for Onegin's shortcomings of character. However, at this stage of his career Onegin certainly seems no worse than anyone else.

This is how the first four, critically important, stanzas work. Pushkin first deposits a clear idea of Onegin's nastiness but immediately subtracts from it in three ways. He has more than redressed the balance.

Why he should choose to do this is a question of substance. There are a number of possible answers. First, Pushkin's own personality. He was instinctively genial, good natured and optimistic; an affectionate interest in people and the untidy bits and pieces of ordinary lives emanates from his work as a whole and particularly from this novel. (This is the major distinction between him and his hero, who has a deep dislike for humanity and for life itself). This attitude sweetens the whole tone of *Eugene Onegin* and is certainly a factor to be reckoned with in the presentation of the hero. Then again, Pushkin knows most of the secrets of characterisation. He is on record as preferring the complex characters of Shakespeare to the splendid caricatures of Molière. It is surely in his interests to invest Onegin with as much complexity as he can. In any case, why take things so seriously? Pushkin prefers badinage to weighty discourse. In his work as a whole this agreeable quality if also a great danger; he fills his stories and poems with such sparkling entertainment that we are disinclined to look deeply into them for serious ideas. Pushkin the lightweight artist is a myth that has had too good a run for its money; it will not be brought down easily. We can begin here and now by taking his characters more seriously than the author's chatty manner suggests we should. Finally, we are left with the idea floated in chapter two. Pushkin is involved with Onegin. He was with him for long periods and at crucial stages. Evidently the hero's harshness prevailed over the poet's greater geniality. In retrospect Pushkin can scarcely feel proud of Onegin and his conduct; could it be that he feels a permanent sense of oblique responsibility for all that happened? Any or all of these reasons may lie behind Pushkin's intriguingly defensive exposition of his best-known hero.

When we first meet Onegin he is 'flying through the dust' in his carriage (one, II); speed is important because he has a long journey ahead. In fact, this is an appropriate introduction to him because we shall soon see that hurrying is his normal way of getting about. Words like *stremglav* (headlong) and *streloy* (arrowlike) are commonly used to mark his progress. It is true that he sometimes has reason to hurry, because he has started out late, as when he goes to the ballet (one, XVII) or turns up for the duel (six, XXV). But he always hurries away, as when leaving for dinner with his friend, Kaverin (one, XVI) or going to the ball. On this latter occasion we have to hurry too, just because he has rushed on ahead: 'We had better hurry along to the ball, to which my Onegin has sped away headlong in his hackney carriage ...' (one, XXVII). Onegin's permanent need to hurry tells us, first, that he is always in too much of a rush to notice what is happening around him in the real world. For this reason he misses out on much that is creative, beautiful and significant – a point that we have made before and shall return to. It also implies that he does not mind in the least putting other people out by arriving late. His arrival at the theatre in the first chapter (XXI) stands as a metaphor for his general attitude and behaviour. Everyone else is there and the warmly anticipated performance has begun. In comes Onegin, late. He tramples over people's feet – can you imagine him apologising? – and then puts on his own performance, ostentatiously staring around the theatre, training his lorgnette on any ladies unknown to him, feeling and no doubt expressing displeasure at what he sees and saluting the men he knows on every side. Incidentally, we know from the following stanza (XXII) that, although he arrived late, he also left early. It is reasonable to presume that he stumbled and grumbled his discourteous way out of the house just as he had entered. Onegin the natural misfit is depicted here. He is not only a late-comer, but a nasty intruder. His arrival at the theatre is ill-timed, inconsiderate and thoroughly disruptive. So are all his arrivals, at his own estate, at the Larins', into the lives of Lensky and Tatyana, and into St Petersburg society. Other people must accommodate him; he will make no attempt at civilised behaviour.

Onegin is a man who lives by cruelty and conquest. His progress is measured by the 'destruction' of his rivals (one, XII) and 'brilliant victories' (one, XXXVI). His method is usually that of biting wit and sarcasm. One line with a particularly villainous sound to it sums up his manner of speaking:

> Как он язвительно злословил   (one, XII)

No four words in English can communicate the venom and vitriol of this line which means 'How caustically he would vent his spite in words'. Its key words, *yazvitel'nyy* and *zlost'* (caustic and spite) are the very ones used elsewhere by Pushkin to describe Onegin's language when they first met:

> Сперва Онегина язык
> Меня смущал; но я привык
> К его язвительному спору,
> И к шутке, с желчью пополам,
> И злости мрачных эпиграмм.   (one, XLVI)

> At first Onegin's language
> Disconcerted me but I got used to
> His caustic way of arguing,
> And to his jokes half shot through with bile
> And to the spitefulness of his epigrams.

Thre can be little doubt that Onegin stands out from all the other sharp-witted young men trying to create an impression in society. His misanthropy takes him always a little beyond decent standards into a realm of outright cruelty and destructiveness which virtually anyone else would find repugnant.

His treatment of Lensky is a case in point. Ostensibly, when they meet, he draws on all his powers of restraint and allows the young man both to speak freely and to form a friendship (of sorts). The most revealing moment in the early part of their relationship, however, comes during the conversation between them on the way back from Onegin's first visit to the Larins, at the start of the third chapter. The conversation, translated into prose (no difficult matter), goes as follows. Onegin speaks first. 'Tell me, which one of them was Tatyana?' [As if he didn't know]. 'Oh, the one who ... came in and sat by the window.' 'Are you really in love with the younger one?' 'What if I am?' 'I'd have chosen the other one if I'd been a poet like you. There's no life in Olga's features, like in a Madonna by Vandyke; she's got a round face, and a fair one, like that stupid moon on that stupid horizon.' Upon which Lensky sulks silently all the way home. This kind of Alcestian frankness on Onegin's part does him no credit. Why is it necessary to spell out in such detail what he sees to be wrong with Olga? To call her decent-looking but stupid (that ugly word repeated for emphasis) and less interesting than her sister is gratuitously rude and provoking. (The enormity of Onegin's conduct is stressed by Nabokov, who suggests that these deliberately insulting remarks could well have led to a duel (vol.3, p.8) − a point that we shall return to). Onegin says what he does, not in the interests of truthfulness but specifically in order to hurt and wound Lensky. On this occasion there is no wit, no obliqueness of any kind, but the direct cruelty of these remarks stays in the mind, confirming what we have heard about his way of speaking. Onegin is clearly galled by Lensky's excited happiness and acts instinctively to attack and destroy that which he cannot have himself. This looks like the beginning of the sequence of events which culminates logically enough in Lensky's death. After seeing him in operation throughout the first chapter, where he is presented in such detail, and overhearing conversations like this, no one should be at all surprised at his later actions. However vicious they may become, they remain in, rather than out of, character.

Onegin's behaviour is based on misanthropic disdain. His

vanity is such that he is convinced of his own superiority
(though Pushkin has already warned us that the superiority
is only imaginary). From this it follows that he does not much
care what people think about him. Both in the city and the
country he shows contempt for normal behaviour and popular
opinion, frequently by doing things that are unusual or un-
acceptable. He defies all expectations and many conventions.
His language, as we have seen, is excessively spiteful. Far
from being a hero of his time, he does none of the things
that might be expected of him. (This idea is well developed
by J.D. Clayton who reminds us that his was 'an age that
ascribed very clear roles to individuals' (*Ice and Flame*, p. 140)).
He does not enter state service, he does not marry and settle
down, he does not join the army, he does not become a
Decembrist; neither does he take up an acceptable alternative
role such as that of a poet. In the country he will not conform
to conventional standards of behaviour, refusing to meet
his neighbours as often as he should, deliberately offending
them by avoiding them and by using impolite expressions in
conversation. No matter how much he may choose to follow
fashion, attend to the necessary minutiae of dress, stroll
down the boulevard in the approved manner, get himself
seen and heard in the right places, Onegin remains a strong
individualist. Oddity, nonconformity, eccentricity – these
are the qualities which were recognised in him and by which
we remember him. His country neighbours have him down as
'a most dangerous eccentric' (two, IV). More significant is
Pushkin's own assessment of Onegin when they first met.
One of the first characteristics which struck him was Onegin's
'Inimitable strangeness', a memorable phrase in Russian
which draws attention to itself by spreading out over a whole
line:

Неподражательная странность   (one, XLV)

All of this amounts to an important aspect of Onegin's
conduct. The more prepared we are to accept nonconformity
as a basic characteristic of his, the more difficult it becomes
to see him as a slave to convention. Yet this is precisely what

many people have argued, indeed taken for granted, in relation to his behaviour during the duel. Onegin's provocative conduct before the duel in monopolising and flirting with Olga was itself a flagrant breach of convention, an unthinkable undertaking for anyone at all sensitive to what the watching world might think of him. In fact, he never became locked into codes of conduct that he could not control. No blank necessity takes him over. He is not a helpless child. On the contrary, he remains his own man, and what he does must be judged in straightforward terms of moral responsibility, the same terms that apply to all of us.

Tatyana Larina

In describing the character of Eugene Onegin we have suggested that hitherto he has been misjudged, the full depth of his depravity and the measure of his personal responsibility having been underestimated. In a similar way we shall have to propose a new evaluation of Tatyana Larina. She too has been touched up by Pushkin's expert brush and her shortcomings have been to some extent shaded out. When examined closely, and with as much objectivity as can be mustered against Pushkin's persuasive lyricism, the character of Tatyana may be shown to include elements of make-believe and inconsistency. To impugn the reputation of the best-loved woman in Russian letters is no way to make new friends; nevertheless some of Tatyana's famous charm may have to be described as spurious. More seriously, she will have to forfeit much of the high standing accorded to her on the grounds of her unassailable moral courage.

The two Tatyanas and two Eugenes

Let us deal first with the one great flaw in the portrayal of Tatyana. In terms of character development she goes too far, too fast. When we take our leave of her in the last stanza of chapter seven it is during the spring of 1822: she is twenty or twenty-one years old. She has gone to Moscow where, gauche and unsettled, she has made a not too promising start. She remains disapproving, uncomprehending and taciturn. She reappears only fourteen stanza later (eight, XIV) after a lapse of two and a half years, married these eighteen months or so and accompanied by her husband. She now occupies a position of pre-eminence. She is moving not just among people of prosperity or good birth, but at the very highest level of Russian society. Pushkin calls those who surround her 'the flower of the capital, high nobility and paragons of fashion' (eight, XXIV). Thus, young as she still is, Tatyana has become one of the most envied and accomplished ladies in the whole of Russia. And how she has grown into the role of society queen. Perfectly attired and poised, attractive, carefree and charming, self-possessed even among the most brilliant of rivals, she has also acquired conversational skills which, only a few months earlier, would have been quite beyond her. She is holding forth with the Spanish ambassador (presumably in French) when Onegin finally identifies her. If we think about this with the kind of cool detachment which the poet's agreeable verses actively discourage, we shall have to conclude that such a precipitate advancement from log cabin almost to White House is a bit too good to be true. We may like the idea of it, and we need it for the sake of the story, but this development lacks logic and must be described as unconvincing.

Although it is not the business of our poet to admit to such a disparity, he does so inadvertently when he himself juxtaposes descriptions of the old and new Tatyana. It could hardly be better put.

> But throughout the evening my Onegin
> Was preoccupied with Tatyana alone,
> Not that shy little girl,
> Lovelorn, poor and simple,
> But the indifferent princess,
> The inaccessible goddess
> Of the luxurious royal Neva.   (eight, XXVII)

In the next stanza the point is made more explicit still through a pointed rhetorical question.

> Who would dare to look for that tender little lass
> In this majestic, this offhand
> Lawgiver of the salons?   (eight, XXVIII)

A good question; who indeed? But it is not the sort of question that is usually asked about chapter eight of the novel. While on the subject of this chapter and its illogicalities, we might as well ask a similar question about the hero, Eugene himself. How far can we believe in his lovelorn collapse? Once again calm consideration may suggest that his falling in love with Tatyana, and particularly the devastating extent of it, is as unconvincing as Tatyana's transformation. In the context of the novel's gathering climax and as recounted by Pushkin it seems acceptable. But it does not flow from the logic of what went before. From what well did Onegin draw the fresh waters of anguished love? It is near to unthinkable that such a soulless, dead person could be re-animated in this way. Once again Pushkin himself says what matters.

> Burnt out ashes will not flare up again   (one, LIX)

And if it was not really love, but a fierce envy of what Tatyana has achieved and, as she herself suggests (eight, XLIV), a desire for scandalous honour brought about by her downfall, then there is still a problem to be resolved. Onegin's lovelorn condition is not that of a scandal-hunting seducer or a mere seeker after forbidden fruits (as Pushkin proposes unconvincingly in eight, XXVII). The poet has described it almost too well. We are privy to the whole gamut of Onegin's experiences as he suffers vexation and disturbed sleep (eight, XXI); counts the hours to the next meeting with Tatyana and stands tongue-tied before her (XXII); chases after her like an adolescent, haunting her house and dying for a touch of her clothing or the chance to pick up her handkerchief (XXX); wastes away, physically ill (XXXI); experiences terrible anxiety (XXXIII); despairs of all hope (XXXIV); locks himself away from that despair (XXXV); recalls his beloved in daydreams (XXXVI); descends into lethargy (XXXVII); collapses into near-madness and almost becomes a poet (perhaps, for Onegin, not dissimilar experiences) (XXXVIII); hibernates from unrequited love and emerges only to rush to see his loved one in the spring (XXXIX). All of this behaviour, which squares not at all with what we could ever have expected from the Onegin that we once knew, is out of all proportion to mere seduction or scandal-seeking. It is *in* proportion to the kind of genuine, heartfelt passion of which we know in our heart of hearts this wreck of a man is incapable. Onegin's onrush of love for Tatyana, so beautifully and persuasively described for us, is another *non sequitur*.

The two rejection scenes

This brings us to one of the most significant misreadings of *Eugene Onegin*, the question of Tatyana's response to Onegin at their final meeting. She rejected him and in doing so established a reputation for moral steadfastness which has lasted down the decades. But this rejection in chapter eight is a tit-for-tat encounter, answering the earlier one in the opposite direction (chapter four). (As Tatyana puts it, acidly, 'Today it's my turn' (eight, XLII).) These two encounters must be taken together.

The first rejection scene apparently provides an example of Onegin acting out of character by resisting the temptation to take advantage of the lovelorn young girl who has approached him. The man who never takes account of the feelings of others is suddenly observed acting unselfishly. He does not string her along, or seduce her, or in any way use her for his own gratification. We must wonder why not. Explanations abound. Pushkin, for example, suggests that his hero resisted temptation out of sheer nobility of spirit:

> You will agree, my reader,
> That our friend acted very decently
> Towards the melancholy Tanya;
> Not for the first time he revealed
> Straightforward nobility of soul ...   (four, XVIII)

That sounds simple enough, but perhaps we should not trust a narrator who is so personally involved. Here is another version of events from our own time. 'A seduction ... would have been ... more natural ... but the artificial canons of society manners restrain Onegin, and he makes his own fate' (Brown, *History of Russian Literature*, p. 78). According to this explanation Onegin did not have to draw on the resources of his own character because, once again, he was taken over and controlled by outside forces. Both of these versions accord with the general view that Onegin was demonstrating self-abnegation. The problem seems to be in deciding why he should do so. But perhaps there is no problem. Is it really true that Onegin acted altruistically? Did he really have any temptation to resist?

Possible clues to Onegin's apparent inconsistency are to be found in the circumstances under which he was living. One thing that is clear is that he was not suffering from sexual deprivation. Passionate love affairs were a thing of the past; he considered them hardly worth the trouble and exertion.

> He no longer fell in love with beautiful women,
> But ran after them any old how;
> If they refused him he was consoled in a moment,
> If they were unfaithful he was glad to take a rest. (four, X)

As to the flickering of physical desire which may have remained in him, there was little difficulty in satisfying it now and then in the locality. Among the delights which he allowed himself while living 'like a hermit' was one unanchoretic pleasure, the occasional 'young, fresh kiss from a white-skinned, dark-eyed girl' (four, XXXIX). This detail, although recorded shortly after the rejection of Tatyana, reminds us of the availability of such local girls for the relief of sexual tension in the brain. It would have been surprising to hear that Onegin did not shop occasionally at this stall.

To all of this we must add a note about Tatyana's physical appearance. Pushkin goes to some lengths to emphasise that she is not a beautiful young woman. The very first thing we learn about her, apart from her name, is that, 'Neither with her sister's beauty, nor with her sister's rosy-cheeked freshness would she have attracted anyone's eyes' (two, XXV). In her later incarnation, despite the advantages, no doubt, of expert cosmetic treatment, she has not changed in this respect. 'No one,' we are told, 'could have called her a beautiful woman' (eight, XV). Whatever else Onegin may have felt *vis-à-vis* Tatyana, it really seems as if there would have been no *frisson* of sexual electricity. And if this was lacking, may we not assume that he simply had no inclination to seduce her?

Even if we accept or discard the question of lascivious interest, there was one good reason for Onegin not to become involved in any way with Tatyana Larina: the clear danger of being ensnared in marriage. This was no remote contingency but a real possibility, already talked of in the neighbourhood. The busiest gossips were saying that a marriage between them had already been arranged and its celebration awaited only the acquisition of fashionable wedding rings (three, VI). Tatyana, while pretending to be annoyed at the gossip, was secretly not averse to the idea. These signals must have been clear to the hero. He can only have considered that the slightest move in her direction, for any reason at all, might draw him inextricably into further talk of marriage. When she approached him, therefore, his first instinct must have been not to see whether anything interesting or gratifying could be got out of this development, but to preserve himself at all costs. There seems to be no question of resisting temptation. Onegin's proclivity to act out of self-interest seems to be as apparent in this set of circumstances as at any other stage of his life that we know about.

Incidentally, the actual words used by Onegin in his rejection of Tatyana (four, XIII−XVI) seem also to have been mis-interpreted. For once, he is less black than painted. When Onegin has finished speaking, Pushkin comments, 'This was the sermon that Eugene preached' (four, XVII). The word 'sermon' (*propoved'*) will be picked up by Tatyana when she recalls the occasion much later (eight, XLIII). And critical opinion in general speaks disparagingly of what the hero said to the heroine. Bayley refers to Onegin's discourse as 'priggish virtuousness' (*Pushkin: A Comparative Study*, p.262). He 'harangues' her, gives her a 'lecture' according to Mirsky (*Pushkin*, pp.142−3); 'lecture' is a word used also by Brown who then claims that, after it, Onegin 'goes away utterly self-satisfied' (*History of Russian Literature*, p. 79), for which it is hard to find any textual justification. In point of fact, there is no lecture, no harangue, no sermon. What the hero says is quite reasonable under the circumstances, and, apart from a few words at the end, it is expressed tactfully. He tells Tatyana that he would like her as well as any other woman for his wife, if he were the marrying kind, which he is not. He admits that, even if he could begin a marriage properly, he would never be able to sustain the role of loving husband. He paints an all too realistic picture of an unhappy domestic scene with a dull, sulking husband unworthy of a solicitous wife, and points this out as a likely future prospect if they were to marry. He admits to a kind of brotherly affection for her and looks forward to a more worthy future love match for Tatyana. Only at the last does he sermonise, and then briefly. He warns her, not without good reason, that she must learn to control herself or she might get into trouble by offering herself to a less understanding man. This is put rather bluntly, even though it needs saying, but the dozen words which come at the end of his speech are scarcely sufficient to turn it into a kind of unpleasant homily. Nor does he go on at length; a couple of hundred words and it is all over. (His address to her occupies exactly four stanzas; hers to him, in chapter eight, will take five and a half). Onegin is considerate enough to reply to Tatyana, when he might have ignored her letter, and to do so face to face, when a return letter would have been so much easier. His tone is gentle; he lets her down lightly. Above all, he tells the truth in every particular. This might well be considered one of his finest moments, one of the rare occasions when − since it does not go against his self-interest anyway − he proves capable of doing a decent thing. The irony is that he has been wrongly castigated for adopting a supercilious attitude on this occasion by those very commentators who, elsewhere, are too anxious to exculpate him from crimes that deserve the severest censure.

And so to the final confrontation between Tatyana and Onegin. It is not quite true to say that, 'Here is the crucial point of the entire novel' (Brown, *History of Russian Literature*,

p. 81), because the death of Lensky is an event of greater substance than any failed love match. Nevertheless, the stance adopted by Tatyana has been crucial in determining her reputation and in deciding what the deepest meaning of the novel might be. The canonised view is that Tatyana feels a resurgence of all her old love for Onegin and only with the greatest difficulty resists a temptation to yield to him in some (unspecified) way. Her rocklike determination to do the right thing thus invests her with exemplary moral awareness and probity. Richard Freeborn speaks for many, but more eloquently than most, when he says, 'What Tatyana asserts ... is the privacy of conscience, the singularity of all moral awareness and certitude, the discovery of the single unique moral self which opposes and withstands the factitious morality of the mass, of society, humanity or the general good' (*Rise of the Russian Novel*, p. 37). There is much to be questioned in all of this. It is by no means certain that Tatyana was in love with Onegin, or that she felt tempted to yield to him any more than he had felt tempted the other way round on the earlier occasion. And if she did not feel so tempted, she did not have to draw on deep reserves of restraint and purity, nor can she claim exemplary moral stature.

The question of her love for Onegin is a tricky one. At first sight her love seems undeniable. Does she not actually admit to Onegin that she loves him? Probably the most famous words of the whole novel come at this point, when she says:

> I love you (why pretend otherwise?),
> But I am given to another man
> And I shall be faithful to him for ever.   (eight, XLVII)

But this 'love' is difficult to believe in. First of all, this declaration itself is stilted and bookish. John Bayley describes it as 'stylised composure' (*Pushkin: A Comparative Study*, p. 262). This is a good description, in view of Tatyana's unencouraging use of the second person plural, followed by a rather forced rhetorical question; compared with Tatyana's effusions in chapter three it has no genuine ring. In any case, why Tatyana should now entertain love for Eugene Onegin is truly hard to understand. She has unmasked him by looking round his house and particularly by going through his books (chapter seven). She has recognised his hollowness; she called him a 'parody' of a man (seven, XXIV). More to the point, she knows that he caused the duel with Lensky and went through with it to the bitter end. He has been thoroughly exposed and cannot now appear to her as the glamorous deliverer that she built up in her imagination nearly five years before. Now, after years of aimless wandering, months of anguish and a winter locked away in hibernation, he can scarcely look, sound or seem a handsome prospect. (He is described as 'looking like a corpse' (eight, XL).) Nor does she believe in his love; she thinks that he is after quick gratification along with a sense of scandalous triumph.

Many people have discovered the obvious truth that Tatyana and Onegin are hopelessly incompatible, and that Tatyana herself understands this. Dostoyevsky admitted that, even if she were to become available, say through widowhood, she would not give herself to Onegin. More recently W.E. Brown has pointed out that, after coming to a proper understanding of him, 'she knows him through and through . . . and realizes their utter incompatibility'; she 'cannot delude herself that she can find happiness with such a man' (*History of Russian Literature*, p.83). But still her love is accepted as real. It is not enough to say, ah, but love is blind and can exist in a person against all reason. This may be so, but if a novelist has to fall back upon such convenient truisms he is defying the logic of his own characterisation and taking too easy a way out. Let us set this at the minimum, without eliminating all possibility of love existing in Tatyana's heart: it is more likely that she either *thinks* she is in love, or else that she *says* she is in love without believing it, than that she really is in love. Or perhaps she is confused and does not quite realise what she is saying.

There is further evidence to suggest that, being deeply moved, she is not thinking clearly or expressing herself accurately at this time. Perhaps the most interesting comment from her comes when she says, only a few words before her 'confession' of love:

> But happiness was so possible,
> So close! ...   (eight, XLVII)

This is not just wrong, it is demonstrably untrue. There was
never a point in the story, except early on and in the imagination
of an impressionable young girl, when happiness linking her
with him was either possible or close. Any kind of a liaison
would have spelt disaster. Yet Tatyana makes that statement
and appears to believe it. The fact is that at this time she is
not in control of herself. A wave of emotion has swept across
her and her thoughts are blurred.

The onset and the nature of this condition can be determined
with some accuracy. Onegin's sudden appearance had the
effect of transporting Tatyana back into her old home and her
former personality.

> ... The simple maid,
> With her dreams and her heart of bygone days,
> Is now resurrected again in her.   (eight, XLI)

From that point on Tatyana exists in two forms, the country
girl and the princess, both personalities jostling for pre-eminence
in her mind. The present-day St Petersburg hostess never loses
complete control, but what Tatyana would really like to do
is turn the clock back and become her old self, bring her
beloved nurse back to life and carry on as before. It is this
old life which she is really in love with rather than the Onegin
who now kneels before her. The old Tanya is in love with
the old Eugene. It is the old Tanya who toys with the idea
that happiness may be both possible and close at hand. The
idea that Princess Tatyana N is in love with the corpselike
Eugene Onegin, with his terrible history, is less convincing
than that the resurrected Tanya is in love with her one-time
hero and the life gone by.

This is not an issue which can be settled definitively. Some
will always maintain that, despite everything, the superficial
story of Princess N being desperately in love with the returning
Onegin is the correct one. What matters more than this,
however, is her decision not to yield to him, about which we
really must come to a decision. On this hangs the whole

question of her enviable reputation for strong-minded morality. The issue can be reduced to a straightforward alternative. If Tatyana was truly tempted to betray her husband by running away with Onegin or by entering into adultery with him, then she deserves all the credit she has been given for resisting that temptation. If not, she does not, and must be thought of otherwise. The facts of the case seem to suggest that Tatyana did not have much temptation to resist. She has seen through Onegin and her own silly infatuation; she cannot fail to remember the virtual murder of Lensky; five years have passed, during which she has matured remarkably. Onegin, on his reappearance, has nothing to offer her at all, beyond the capacity to re-evoke memories of a lost way of life. For her to contemplate elopement with him is a ludicrous idea. A platonic relationship beyond their present one would be without meaning, and in any case Onegin is asking for more than that. We are left only with the possibility of an illicit sexual union. This is what Tatyana has to decide about.

Circumstances suggest both that Onegin is too unattractive a proposition and that Tatyana would have too much to lose by taking such a risk for her to have lingered more than a moment over her decision. In rejecting him she takes the *easy and obvious* decision rather than the one that presents heartbreaking difficulty. She also gives the novel a relatively happy ending in which Onegin gets what he deserves (or does not get what he does not deserve), and she lives on in sufficient prosperity to provide compensation for the need to live a life that would not have been her first choice. There is some sadness in all this but no sense of tragedy, particularly because of the embarrassment which follows immediately, upon the arrival of Tatyana's husband, and the casual way in which the narrator quickly takes his leave. This is why Tchaikovsky had to add something to the ending of his operatic version. The contrast between the two works, clearly marked in this closing scene, is nicely summarised by Gary Schmidgall: 'While "Onegin" ends with a rollicking envoi, the opera ends with Onegin's last tragic words – there are none in the poem – and the fortissimo rush of chords that announce so many operatic catastrophes' (*Literature as Opera*, p. 229).

The two rejection scenes are unusually similar. In both of them the temptation to accept a proposal rather than reject it is illusory; rejection is the proper course and one which is not all that difficult to follow. An awareness of this changes our perception of the two main characters, underlining consistency in Onegin's case, detracting from high moral standing in Tatyana's.

The earlier Tatyana

So far we have dealt mainly with the mature Tatyana, the imperious, law-giving hostess of the St Petersburg salon and ballroom. But the Tatyana beloved by every last Russian-reader is the earlier one, the innocent young girl who falls in love. Here we shall not attempt to be iconoclastic. Many of the scenes in which Tatyana appears really are among the most memorable and lovable in Russian literature − for that matter, in any literature. In particular the five stanzas in chapter three in which Tatyana first articulates her love in the presence of her nurse, Filatyevna (XVI−XX), have enough tender beauty in them to move the hardest heart. Perhaps there is no passage in the novel which more clearly demonstrates Pushkin's captivating skill. Such a comment is only ninety per cent complimentary because there is much duplicity in this narrator. He writes so as to leave little freedom for independent response; what begins in entertainment proceeds through the gentlest of manipulation and ends with subjugation to the poet's will. This particular extract demonstrates the process well.

Here we have a moonlit scene *par excellence*. It is all unreality, but every reader will believe every word of it. Intellect and memory will protest in vain that Eugene Onegin is a hopeless match for Tatyana. It is no good bearing in mind even Pushkin's warning to the young girl as recently as the previous stanza: 'Tatyana, my dear Tatyana! I weep tears with you ... You will perish, my dear girl ...' (three, XV).

All of this simply dissolves when Pushkin turns on the full effects of his love poetry. Tatyana goes out into the garden, indirectly invokes the reassuring power of the patrolling moon, and we are lost. From then on, instead of squirming at the prospect that lies ahead for the young girl, we believe in her love and share her aching desire for a positive response to it. We simply want young love to succeed. It is the gentle beauty of the scene which impresses the reader, and stays with him, rather than any sense of wrongness or danger.

This kind of enchantment can be worked only through the most excellent poetry. Pushkin makes a series of astoundingly good decisions. He will avoid straightforward narrative or reflective monologue, and do most of his work through dialogue – after all, this is a novel. He will balance one thing with another: youth with age, soaring lyricism with earthly responses, laconism with wordiness, implied thoughts with articulated speech, the distant past with the immediate present, abstract ideas with tangible, ordinary objects. He will deliberately digress and even interpolate a story within a story, risking the reader's impatience while winding him up in suspense. He will allow himself, by his normal standards, a lot of room: five stanzas, seventy lines, more than three hundred words. The complicated formula works well.

The first stanza (three, XVI) is a decided risk. We are conducted into the garden where the heroine is suddenly overtaken with an ardent passion. Burning sexuality is suggested by Tatyana's lowered eyes, rising bosom and flushed cheeks; we come near to melodramatic overstatement with a singing in her ears and lights flashing before her eyes; triteness and sentimentality seem to join hands in presenting the moon, the dark trees and the nightingale, a bird which Nabokov reminds us 'has been to countless poets what the rose is among flowers' (vol. 2, p. 361). The poet seems to have invited all his enemies to this feast, but none of them will prevail. It is a dependable certainty that when Pushkin verges upon excess he does so either in the interests of parody or because he is about to move to the opposite extreme, to come right down to earth. The latter happens here. He has ventured the extravagant, knowing first that this is appropriate to Tatyana's highly emotional state of mind, and also that he can follow it with the prosaic in such a way that the balance will come out about right. The last two lines of the stanza contain ten very ordinary words nicely bridging the gap between the exaggeratedly poetic setting of the garden scene and the ensuing dialogue.

> Татьяна в темноте не спит
> И тихо с няней говорит.   (three, XVI)

> In the darkness Tatyana cannot sleep
> And quietly she talks to her nurse.

The quiet conversation is where the real charm begins. Tatyana's breathless excitement would have carried her over the brink into torrential expostulations of love. The presence of her nurse ensures that her feet stay on the ground. But the real secret of poetic success here is the natural way in which Pushkin fits normal-seeming dialogue to the unaccommodating iambic tetrameter. This is one of those (plentiful) sections of the poem where the verses could be laid out in prose without any change to the word order. Imagine this to be a play; the speakers would proceed as follows:

TATYANA: I can't sleep, nanny. It's so stuffy here! Open the window and come and sit over here with me.
NURSE: Why, Tanya, what's the matter with you?
TATYANA: I feel depressed. Let's talk about the olden days.
NURSE: What about them, Tanya? Time was, I used to store up in my memory such a lot of ancient stories and fables about evil spirits and young maidens, but now it's all gone dark, Tanya. I've forgotten what I used to know. Oh yes, bad times are on us! I get confused.
TATYANA: Nanny, tell me about your old times. Did you ever fall in love in those days?   (three, XVII)

And so it goes on, for another lovely thirty-two lines. The melody of the prose dialogue is beautifully orchestrated in the rich underlying poetry. Unnoticed, the iambic rhythm flows by, the quiet rhymes come and go in their intricate arrangements, and the sounds play about in pleasing patterns. Much could be made of this but we shall look at a single example. The nurse's diction in stanza XVII not only contains a memorably euphonious line in

> Старинных былей, небылиц
>
> Ancient stories and fables

but also sets up earlier and later resonances with two similar vowels, both the throaty 'ы' ('y') and its soft counterpart 'и' ('i'). In a delightful series of recapitulations we hear, '*byvalo ... khranila ... starinnykh byley, nebylits ... zlykh ... devits ... nynche ... zabyla ... zashiblo*'. Not only is this sound patterning intrinsically pleasing, it is also, with its seven husky 'y' vowels, appropriate to the hoarse old voice which is supposed to be producing it. What appears to be prose is actually the busiest of poetry. The colloquial Russian does not slip, the different registers remain true between the two speakers, not a single tortured victim is claimed by the tyrants who normally maintain despotic rule over word order, line-ends, stanza-ends and especially rhyme. Without gloating over their inadequacy, it is particularly revealing to glance at some of the English translations of this passage. We can use a few unPushkinian examples from them to make it clear what the Russian poet avoids in the way of fractured speech. He could never have brought himself to say the Russian equivalent of 'The matchmaker a fortnight sped, Her suit before my parents pressing'; 'Nurse, of thy youth I would be told'; 'I lived, by strangers quite surrounded'; 'I hadn't fourteen summers yet. The broker-woman came applying Around my kin two weeks'; or 'So I'd spend my hours in fear and bitter crying'. Fluent, natural dialogue is one of the striking features of *Eugene Onegin* in general; in this passage it is seen at its best.

The contrast between the young girl and the old nanny is exquisite. Breathless and fluttering soprano alternates with croaky contralto. (Although, curiously, in Tchaikovsky's opera the contralto role goes to Olga, and the nurse is sung at mezzo-soprano level). A surprising feature is that the old lady takes up three times as much space as her young charge. She rambles on, telling the story of her own marriage which holds tantalising interest for us in terms of personal destiny, social history and human relations in general. We are torn between listening to this marvellous recitation and enjoying all its fascinating details – she married at thirteen and her husband was even younger! – and allowing our attention to drift off after Tatyana, who has probably heard it all before and, in any case, has other things on her mind. Didn't she ask about love? When are we going to get back to that? The sweet build-up of suspense, the endearing niceness of both participants, the palpable separation between the chatter and the thinking, the openness and warm intimacy, the pressing importance of all that is said and not said – these qualities create a passage of memorable content expressed in immaculate style.

The tension is temporarily resolved at the beginning of stanza XIX when the old nurse realises what we already know, that Tatyana is not listening. Then follows a further slight delay, rapidly putting on the pressure again, while Filatyevna explores the improbable idea that her little girl is ill. Anyone who has simultaneously suffered and enjoyed such ministrations from a loving old person will recognise the authenticity of this little digression, and also the spluttering amazement which she suffers when the child suddenly becomes a young woman by saying she is in love. Filatyevna's instinctive reaction is to make the sign of the cross with her thin hand and to start praying for Tatyana. These words and deeds are a mixture of truth, love and humour, the beautiful quality of which is uncommon even in Pushkin. The details are worth lingering over; enjoyable as they are in their own right, they will also defer the real interest and thus build up suspense. Tatyana, naturally enough, loves the sound of her love. She breathes out the words 'I am in love' three times, at three different speeds, in three different tones, leaping within half a dozen words from timidity to triumph.

All that is left is for Pushkin to escort us down from this peak of poetic ecstasy. He does so by pointing out one or two incidental attractions as we descend. Here is Tatyana with her dishevelled hair, the picture of restless young femininity, tremendously aroused and scarcely in control of itself. There is the garden bench, and on it the old nurse in her scarf and body-warmer. The wood, the cotton, the padding may seem gratuitous; they are indispensable, keeping illusion wrapped up in reality. And then the recognisable world is again enveloped in unreality as we subside into the gentle loveliness of the silent night and its moonscape:

И все дремало в тишине
При вдохновительной луне.   (three, XX)

And in the stillness everything slumbered
In the light of the inspirational moon.

Our small story has completed its cycle from moon to moon, with another ambrosial phrase (*Pri vdokhnovitel'noy lune*) to end on. What reader, emerging from five stanzas of such enchantment, can have preserved any sense of logic or reason, particularly in relation to Tatyana? At the end of *A Midsummer Night's Dream* what witness will bring choplogic to bear upon the similarly named Titania? The two moonlit worlds are not dissimilar.

This discussion shows two things: in general, how Pushkin's persuasive narrative manner functions and, more specifically, how Tatyana is characterised. When the world falls in love with Tatyana it has ceased to deal with the introverted, emotionally deprived, unintelligent, indeed rather silly creature who is actually depicted in the novel. At the same time it has conveniently forgotten that she has fallen in love with a totally unsuitable partner who could never bring her within smiling distance of happiness. (How different this is from Juliet's love for Romeo, who is unsuitable for her only in political terms). What the world has done is to renew its affection for youth, beauty, dreams and love itself, in which it wishes passionately to believe and is persuaded to believe by the captivating force of good poetry.

Can it be fair to describe the actual, rather than the perceived, character of Tatyana in such disparaging terms? Most people would not do so. Take the question of intelligence. Would anyone who knows and loves Tatyana balk at the description of her as 'intelligent, shy and awkward' (Brown, *History of Russian Literature*, p. 81)? But we have called her the opposite, unintelligent and even rather silly. When you look closely at what she does and says it is difficult to maintain a belief in the quality of her bright mind and capacity for reasoning. Her intellect serves her badly, resulting in a series of misreadings and misjudgements. She takes literature for real life. She meets what will prove to be a wreck of a man and sees him as a kind of hero, or at least a God-sent guardian. She has more warning of the duel than anyone else − her vision of Eugene's capacity for violence, vouchsafed only to her, gives her an advantage over other people who had only the normal warning signs to go on − but she fails to see it coming and thus cannot prevent it. Even after this, when Onegin has departed, she tries to understand him not on the basis of his recent behaviour but through his personal possessions, especially his books. Her habit of placing greater credence in stories than in facts is perpetuated; thus she describes him as a parody (seven, XXIV) when she should be calling him a murderer. Even after her transformation into a grand lady in the last chapter she misreads the signals and wrongly interprets his love, which is genuine, as a desire for her scandalous dishonour. It has to be said that if there is one quality which Tatyana does not possess in large measure it is intelligence. (The only character in the story who could probably be described as intelligent is Lensky, who was earmarked for study abroad at an early age, but gets little credit for it).

Much of what Tatyana stands for is silly and dangerous. But this does not mean that she is not a proper heroine for our novel. She has colour, fierce independence, passion, courage, imagination and initiative. There is about her an aura of something excitingly different. Pushkin himself, her first and greatest admirer, has trouble in explaining what it is. At first he can only tell us what she is not; she enters the story as the heroine of a dozen negatives (in stanzas XXV– XXVII of chapter two). The phrase that suits her best is the one which we have already seen applied to Onegin, 'Inimitable strangeness' (one, XLV), except that Onegin's strangeness puts others in danger whereas, in her strangeness, Tatyana poses a threat only to herself.

Tatyana's greatest single quality is her intuition. Unreliable though this elusive attribute may be, it produces her one real triumph, manifested in her dream. This marvellous excursion, occupying just over ten stanzas (XI–XXI) at the beginning of chapter five has been the subject of much speculation, especially in this century. The exegetes and symbolists have feasted upon it. The most reasonable explanation of the dream comes from R. A. Gregg, who points out that there are two dreams, not one. The first depicts Tatyana in a snowy wilderness, surprised, led, pursued and then assisted by a bear. The second shows a gang of weird monsters around a table in a hut, with Eugene Onegin in their midst; when they threaten her he asserts himself as their master and claims her for himself. At the end of this second dream Olga and Lensky enter, Onegin stabs Lensky to death after a loud argument, and the whole scene erupts in chaos.

It is not stretching things too far to see the bear as a future husband, unwanted (because Tatyana cannot have Onegin), threatening, but essentially harmless, the monsters as the guests who are about to arrive for the name-day party and Onegin as himself, finally claiming her. Most critics accept what is obvious, that the dream is also an expression of Tatyana's sexuality. Whereas a later commentator will take this idea to an offensive extreme, suggesting the theme of masturbation (Clayton, 'Towards a feminist reading', pp. 264–5), Gregg keeps it within bounds. His proposal that the two dreams establish a connection 'between Tatyana's self-imputed sin (illicit desire) and her imagined punishment (rape)' seems coherent and sensible ('Tat'iana's two dreams', p. 505). But the most important detail in the entire dream sequence is Tatyana's perception of Onegin. She assesses him as dominant, destructive and a bitter enemy of Lensky. The murder of Lensky by Onegin should not be considered a prediction; it is an intuition of Onegin's real character and potential, as well as his true attitude to Lensky. All the characters in the story (and most commentators upon it) have taken the superificial friendship between the two young men more or less at face value; in fact, there is neither tolerance nor friendship on Onegin's side, but only the bitterest envy. Tatyana seems to have understood this before anyone else. The trouble is that her secret knowledge remains hidden in the depths of her subconscious mind.

Tatyana is the one really complicated and mysterious character in *Eugene Onegin*. The mystery arises from her own perverse individuality, and particularly from a shroud of awkward contradictions in which she is enveloped. She is not admirable, beautiful or intelligent, but she remains utterly charming. She is ranged against the most unsuitable partner imaginable, yet for much of the time we more than half want the match to succeed. She emerges unscathed, prosperous and much compensated for any disappointments which she may have suffered, yet the image of a tragic heroine persists. But the mystery can be explained. One of the most sensitive and knowledgeable of all Russian critics, Prince Dmitri Mirsky, gives us the key to it. Generously acknowledging the disparity between the two Tatyanas, which we have already discussed, he says, 'We do not, as a rule, remark this [inconsistency] ... we see each half-Tatiana in terms of the whole Tatiana ... We have obeyed the poet, but we have done so because we have been fascinated by his lyrical power, not because we have weighed the objective evidence ...' (*Pushkin*, p.151). This is one of the most revealing statements ever made in relation to Tatyana and, incidentally, to the novel as a whole. Mirsky has described the exact process by which the strange young country girl has been transformed into a national heroine, and by which many misconceptions about her adventures have arisen. Pushkin really has seduced us into a realm of illusion. We go with him willingly. One miraculously effective 'sonnet' stanza succeeds another and all we want is more. When this poet is telling the story, who has the slightest interest in the 'objective evidence'?

Chapter 4

Olga, Lensky and the duel

The most fully authenticated characters in *Eugene Onegin* are Onegin and Tatyana. Nevertheless, important roles are played also by the more thinly drawn Lensky and Olga, to whom we must now turn.

The younger sister

Olga appears in only about twenty stanzas, a third of the space devoted to Lensky, and she does not develop sufficient interest or complexity to detain the critical eye for long. She does not actually do very much, her role being to react to others and to be there in the background as an important reference point. Lensky is partly defined by her slender personality; he is so easily satisfied, indeed transported, by her childish charms that we must account him little more than a boy himself. Everything about Olga is obvious: her physical appearance, her passion, her innocence, her uncomprehending attitude and naive acceptance of everything, down to the rapid transference of her affection to a soldier quite soon after Lensky's death.

Critics have done her a disservice by taking her too seriously. Sometimes she is merely rejected in passing with disparaging epithets such as 'doll-like ... the very pattern of a mindless country miss' (Brown, *History of Russian Literature*, p. 81). Sometimes she is more roundly criticised for being 'temperamentally incapable of not responding to [Onegin's] attention' (Bayley, *Pushkin: A Comparative Study*, p. 257), or for a 'failure to observe her duty to her betrothed' (Freeborn, *Rise of the Russian Novel*, p. 31). She and Lensky are condemned for 'their artificiality, their tawdriness and their insincerity' (Fennell, *Nineteenth-century Russian Literature*,

p. 48). J. D. Clayton hints unrealistically at her probable sexual awareness, even spotting 'an easily perceptible phallic quibble' in Lensky's pen (*Ice and Flame*, pp. 132−3), and heaps exegetic material upon poor Olga so that she becomes 'not a character but a cliché ...' (p. 131), 'a mass of clichés: a blonde, blue-eyed, ruddy-complexioned Helen masquerading as a Madonna' (p. 135). Perhaps Pushkin is really to blame; he started it all by castigating Olga both for her ordinariness (two, XXIII) and for unfaithfulness to the memory of Lensky (seven, X). All of this is unfair.

The truth is that Olga is sixteen years old when we first meet her, she may be seventeen at the time of the duel and perhaps just eighteen when she marries her soldier. She is pretty and vivacious. When she leaves home the sound of her ringing voice is what they most miss. She seems rather a nice little creature and it is clearly too much to expect her to be perceptive and serious with so little experience of the world. Mindless she may or may not be − we cannot tell from the snapshot portrait given to us − but she is likely to do at least as well as these more interesting people whose misapprehensions and mistakes will create such havoc in their own lives and in the lives of others.

Vladimir Lensky

Much of what we have said about Olga applies also to Lensky, but on a grander scale. He is only seventeen when we first meet him and he will die well before his nineteenth birthday. Lensky's age is disputed by Nabokov, who feels he must be older, perhaps twenty or even twenty-one. Nabokov's confusion on this question is not without interest. At one point he asks, 'How old was Lenski? Surely, not seventeen to eighteen, as suggested ...' (vol. 3, p. 17) and he goes on to point out that when Benjamin Constant's Adolphe finished at Göttingen university (from where Lenski has just returned) he was twenty-two. Elsewhere, however, the same author says: 'It is amusing to note that the fictional Vladimir Lenski is the second Göttingen student to be Onegin's friend: the first was

Kaverin ... who, in terms of historical reality, finished his studies there at seventeen, Lenski's age' (vol. 2, p. 229). All of this should count in Lensky's favour since Nabokov also points out that the youngsters who were sent to foreign universities at fourteen or fifteen were 'gifted boys'; perhaps this is a real clue to Lensky's actual quality. But the point tends to be forgotten, along with an awareness of Lensky's young age at the time of his relationship with Onegin. Nabokov's mysterious attempt to age Lensky looks like wishful thinking on his part. He would have liked Lensky to be older, so that Onegin's slaying of him would look a little less brutal. But the text contains two references, consistent with each other, strongly suggesting the seventeen to eighteen age-range (two, X and six, X).

Once again we must accuse Pushkin of starting the anti-Lensky tradition. In fact, he could scarcely have started it more promptly, beginning as he does with a joke even as the young man is introduced.

> По имени Владимир Ленский,
> С душою прямо геттингенской...   (two, VI)

> By name Vladimir Lensky,
> With a soul truly Göttingen-like ...

The macaronic rhyme *Lensky/Gettingenskoy* is a comic masterpiece, one of the most unusual, eye-catching and satisfying in the whole of *Eugene Onegin*. But what a time to deploy it! Poor Lensky can never recover from an introduction like this. With one of his best jokes Pushkin signals to us that we should not take this young person very seriously; first and foremost, he is a figure of fun. (In order to make this point clear we have only to remember the easy informality with which he presented Onegin to us (one, II), suggesting warm friendliness. A reversal of these introductions would be unthinkable). It is not only the funny sound of the word *Gettingenskoy* that counts; the meaning of it also ridicules Lensky by hinting vaguely at things abstract, Romantic and unRussian. The same stanza ends, incidentally, in another joke. Delineating the assets which the newcomer has brought with him from 'foggy Germany' Pushkin refers to 'the fruits of learning, freedom-loving daydreams, an ardent and rather unusual spirit' and also

> Всегда восторженную речь
> И кудри черные до плеч.   (two, VI)

> Ever enthusiastic speech
> And black curls down to his shoulders.

The gushing chatter and eye-catching black curls speak for themselves. The silliness which they imply is underlined, once again, by splendid rhyming. To rhyme *rech '* with *plech* is to use two nouns, but with a feminine accusative singular (plus soft-sign) set against a neuter genitive plural (with no soft-sign, though still providing a perfect rhyme). This is about as far as one could go in stretching the distance between two similar parts of speech. Rhymes with crossed grammar like this are particularly striking; Pushkin's minor triumph of rhyming virtuosity itself trembles on the edge of a little joke. But the real humour comes from bathos in the last line, when a physical characteristic (and a slightly amusing one, since long black curls would be rather outrageous in that setting) suddenly runs up to tag itself on to a sequence of spiritual and intellectual qualities. All in all, this must be considered one of Pushkin's cleverest stanzas; what we need to understand is that behind the amusement lies an intention to undermine the standing of Vladimir Lensky.

This is by no means the end of it. As it happens, the same two technical devices, macaronic rhyming and bathos in the terminal couplet, will soon be used again. Three stanzas on we learn that Vladimir is a poet, drawing his inspiration from the Germans.

> Он с лирой странствовал на свете
> Под небом Шиллера и Гете ...   (two, IX)

> He wandered the world with his lyre;
> Under the skies of Schiller and Goethe ...

Who could read these lovely lines, with their hilarious linking of *svete* with the fractured Russian version of Goethe's hallowed name, without a smile? The trouble is that, while the joke does nothing to demean the two German poets with their unassailable reputations, it does reiterate the silliness of Lensky, particularly in attempting to emulate them. The next stanza is the one with a second example of bathos at the end. After reciting some of the high-flown subjects adopted by the young poet in his verses — pure love, the sadness of parting, vaguely felt emotions, and so on — Pushkin concludes with this couplet:

> Он пел поблеклый жизни цвет
> Без малого в осьмнадцать лет.   (two, X)

> He sang of life's faded blossom
> At not quite eighteen years of age.

These apparently trivial details matter a good deal. Pushkin could have presented Lensky otherwise, perhaps by making more of his probable giftedness. This is how he chose to do it, by gently ridiculing him from the start, making him seem particularly silly.

Take the matter of poetry. Lensky's verses are unoriginal and cliché-ridden; we can scarcely remain ignorant of this since some of them are included in the text. Pushkin has mysteriously come across the lines written by the anguished Lensky on the eve of the duel. It would have been kinder to pass over them with a brief description, but the narrator thinks it necessary to parade them verbatim. They are not good; Pushkin is right to call them, disparagingly, 'Romanticism', 'filled with the nonsense of love' (six, XXIII and XXI). To make matters worse our accomplished poet then proceeds to ridicule Lensky even further at the very moment of his death. Nabokov has observed shrewdly that the lines immediately following the young man's collapse (six, XXXI, lines 10−14) amount to a 'torrent of unrelated images ... a deliberate accumulation of conventional poetic formulas by means of which Pushkin mimics poor Lenski's own style' (vol.3, p.52). Worse still, when writing his final lines Lensky is reported as having read some Schiller before taking up the pen himself. Not allowed to rest quietly in his mediocrity as a versifier, he is always being compared to real poets — Goethe, Schiller and, perhaps inevitably, Pushkin himself. All of which makes him look absurd. How different our perception of Lensky would have been if Pushkin had chosen to compare him not with great fellow writers but with the majority of people, who cannot write at all. Why not compare him with Eugene Onegin? Here is a man who has not an iota of poetry in him and cannot write anything, even though he has tried (one, XLIII). In fact, he cannot even *read* anything (one, XLIV). By contrast, Lensky could have been made to seem full of sensitivity and potential; he could certainly have been presented in a positive light. However, we have what we have. Lensky cannot take a step without seeming to be sillier than he really is.

We are, of course, accusing Alexander Pushkin of bias. It is not that he likes Onegin and dislikes Lensky, but he certainly supports the former, perhaps because he is in awe and slightly afraid of him, and he reduces the latter. Amiable it may be, but his attitude is still one of denigration. The best illustration of this preferential treatment will be found in Pushkin's attitude to the pair of them immediately after the duel. He speculates about Lensky's future, if only he had lived. Perhaps he would have become a great poet, suggests our narrator in a sarcastic stanza (six, XXXVII), knowing that we shall immediately discount this impossibility. The only other future envisaged for Lensky is to have abandoned the muse, to have married and become cuckolded and then to have descended, bored, into fat, gouty middle-aged weariness. We are left to conclude that nothing pleasant or successful was likely to have happened to such an unpromising youngster. By contrast, the monster who has just murdered Lensky is treated with sympathetic leniency. Pushkin says he will tell us what happened to everyone after the duel:

> But not now. Though with all my heart
> I love my hero,
> Though I shall return to him, of course,
> I can't be bothered with him just now. (six, XLIII)

This is a shocking moment. Even Nabokov, who has no time for the callow Lensky and who explains Onegin's vile crime as being out of character, cannot resist the following comment on Pushkin's ill-chosen words: 'There is something pleasantly grotesque about this declaration of love for one's hero when one has just dispatched poor Lenski' (vol. 3, p. 62). Grotesque, perhaps; pleasant, perhaps not. At all events, Alexander Sergeyevich has put his cards on the table. We know what he is doing, and it is not too difficult to understand why. The mocking tone with which Lensky is introduced, described and eventually dispatched is there for an important reason: to mitigate the guilt of Onegin. If the victim can be shown, through ridicule, to be inconsequential, the murderer comes to look less blameworthy. Conversely, if Lensky had been portrayed as a nice young chap, if a little on the naive side as yet, full of sound intellect, genuine feeling and good intentions, a healthy presence and a force of good, with every chance of a decent and happy life ahead of him − all of which appears to be perfectly possible, though one would hardly guess it − then Onegin would have appeared as a figure of greater iniquity. This is the strategy, and it has proved successful.

Not that the critics have deluged Lensky with disparaging comments. We have already seen him dismissed, along with Olga, as 'artificial', 'tawdry' and 'insincere' (Fennell, *Nine-teenth-century Russian Literature*, p. 48). Belinsky saw him as a man inevitably destined for complete philistinism or old-fashioned mysticism, either way an enemy of progress (Hoisington, *Russian Views*, p. 42). W. E. Brown refers to his 'ominous potentiality', though this turns out to be nothing more than a suggestion that Lensky is 'fettered to the society he rejects' (*History of Russian Literature*, p. 81). Richard Freeborn claims that he must take his share of the blame for the 'ensuing events' (including, presumably his own death) because of his 'failure to make a balanced judgement' (*Rise of the Russian Novel*, p. 31). But this is about as far as it goes. The critics have erred not so much in denigrating young Lensky as in brushing him and his concerns smilingly to one side. He has been consigned to the margin, dismissed as irrelevant to the main story. He does not matter very much. It is possible to sketch the story-line of *Eugene Onegin* without even mentioning him. The two different Penguin translations of the novel manage to do this in both introductions. John Bayley we have already quoted (see p. 28 above); before him Avram Yarmolinsky summarises things as follows: 'Onegin's maladjustment ... may be interpreted as a protest against the slave-owning society of which he was the product ... The story of Eugene and Tatyana is at bottom a story of failure and wasted lives. The man obviously runs into a dead end. The woman ... is clear-eyed enough to perceive the weakness of the man she loves ...' (Deutsch translation, p. 14). Poor Lensky. He whose life was wasted more than anyone else's gets no mention. By any objective standards there is only one event of real consequence in this novel, and that is the death of this young man, but we are persuaded otherwise. It is as though, compared with the Onegin–Tatyana relationship, the duel did not have great significance; it could almost be forgotten. As F.D. Reeve puts it, bluntly: 'The death is incidental' (*The Russian Novel*, p. 19). This is an authorial conjuring trick, as morally wrong as it is successful. The enormity of Pushkin's achievement can be appreciated only by looking closely at the duel and at the apologetic attitude which most critics have adopted towards Onegin's role in it.

The duel

The basic facts of the duel between the eighteen-year-old Lensky and the twenty-five-year-old Onegin are clear. Early on the morning of 14 January 1821 the two men depart for the duelling ground. Lensky arrives at the appointed time, which we may presume to be 7 a.m. Onegin arrives about two hours later, having overslept. No attempts at reconciliation are made. Although some of the normal conventions of duelling are being infringed – Onegin has brought no witness and no person who would normally be considered suitable as a second – the two combatants exchange a few gruff words and agree to begin at once. Lensky's second, Zaretsky, marks out a track of thirty-two paces and, at his signal, the two opponents approach each other. Onegin walks four paces forward and then takes aim at Lensky's upper body. They move on a further five paces, by which time Lensky is beginning to aim himself. But he is too late; Onegin fires when they are fourteen paces apart and Lensky is killed instantly, shot through the chest. (Incidentally, Pushkin and d'Anthès were slightly closer when the Russian poet was mortally wounded. It is worth while pacing these distances out in the garden to get a good idea of what is going on; anyone who does so will appreciate that Onegin had Lensky well within accurate shooting range).

It is obvious who has the advantage throughout these proceedings. Onegin is seven years older than his inexperienced adversary and he has fought duels before. In chapter one we discovered that, some time before, he had lost all taste for 'fighting with sword and lead' (one, XXXVII), which suggests a good deal of experience, perhaps in several capacities. To make matters worse, he has kept Lensky waiting for two hours. The effect of this delay is easy to imagine, both in terms of the disconcerting anguish which the young man must have undergone and in relation to his physical condition. After standing around for two hours out of doors on a January morning just after sun-up he can scarcely have been in any condition to hold a weapon, let alone fire it accurately. In any case, Onegin's behaviour has been so unconventional – in appointing his manservant as second and leaving all the formalities to Zaretsky while the wretched Guillot hides behind a tree-stump – that poor Lensky must have wondered what on earth was going on.

Even ignoring the fact of a practised duellist confronting a tyro, the circumstances of this match are so wrong, so outrageously tilted in favour of the stronger man, that it simply should never have been allowed to go ahead. The trouble is that Lensky could hardly protest on his own behalf without looking cowardly. Zaretsky has much to answer for; in fact, it is almost incomprehensible that he did not intervene on Lensky's behalf. Perhaps he was about to do so, but he was given little opportunity. Onegin knows he is breaking the rules by offering only Guillot as a second, but he anticipates any objections and waffles them away in advance. At that point Zaretsky, taken aback, bites his lip, obviously full of misgivings (six, XXVII). This is the moment when the protest should have been articulated. Onegin will not have it. Before even the veteran Zaretsky can collect his wits and do the proper thing, he kills the possibility with a quick, 'Shall we get them started, then?', to which his bewildered opponent can only say yes. It is scarcely an exaggeration to claim that, in pushing ahead under all these circumstances, Onegin is actually cheating.

Let us work back through the various stages of the duel, considering what happened and what might have happened. The firing of the fatal shot merits close scrutiny. It is Onegin who takes aim first, after only four paces, and straight at Lensky's chest. His aim is early, long and deliberate. Lensky's shock, on seeing this, is easy to imagine. He must have realised suddenly that Onegin, although not the offended party, was in deadly earnest. Until that moment it must have seemed improbable that the duel would have a fatal outcome. Imagining the circumstances in advance, Lensky had foreseen that the contestants would 'aim either at the thigh or the temple' (six, XII). Surely the former would be the very worst that could happen. But no, here is Onegin playing it with deadly seriousness. Presumably Lensky would have been about to follow Onegin's lead and aim for a vital organ. The important point is that he takes no initiative himself; Onegin dictates everything, as he has done throughout. Nabokov is quite unfair in assuming that, 'Lenski, no doubt, has murderous intentions ... (vol. 3, p. 41). For this there is no evidence. On balance, it seems more probable that Lensky had no duel plan at all and was going to take his lead from the instigator of all this trouble, who had the power to set its seriousness at any level and could surely be counted on not to push things to the limit. Incidentally, Lensky's instant death may have been due to his adoption of the wrong walking posture. He was shot through the upper abdomen (see six, XXXII), which would have been less accessible if, like a seasoned duellist, he had presented a narrowed profile by walking sideways on with his right arm extended.

Onegin's deliberate aim is the crucial matter in this whole story. Even within the bounds of convention, which are commonly held to be controlling matters at this stage, there was a wide range of possibilities open to him. Zaretsky's gossiping tongue had to be stopped, presumably by the vindication of Onegin's honour. What could Onegin have done? In the first place, he could have apologised and suggested a reconciliation. This possibility really did exist. When people had learned of it subsequently they could hardly have believed that the experienced duellist had been afraid of his greenhorn opponent; instead of accusing Onegin of cowardice they would be more likely to credit him with sparing a young lad from wounding or death. Nevertheless, it is normally assumed that this way out was barred to Onegin. Even if it was, there remained a choice of actions which would have saved his honour and silenced any gossip without the need to kill Lensky. He could have allowed Lensky the first shot, with a strong possibility that the ball would miss him by a mile. Firing either first or second, he could have shot into the air. This would have been the best course of action, proclaiming his honour, courage and disdain for danger and even life itself. If public opinion really mattered, as was suggested by Pushkin at an earlier stage (six, XI), this is what Onegin would have decided upon. He could have reserved his fire. Or he could have taught the young puppy a lesson by aiming no higher than the thigh. We are faced with the stark fact that Onegin refused all of these, and perhaps other, solutions; he went deliberately for the fatal shot.

What needs to be decided now is whether this kind of conduct was, or was not, an aberration on Onegin's part. Nabokov is his greatest champion in this respect. In his eagerness to exculpate Onegin he claims variously that he was behaving 'oddly (i.e., out of tune with the mentality given him by his maker in previous chapters ...)' (vol. 3, pp. 16–17); that he was in a dreamlike state, 'as if he had been infected by Tatiana's recent nightmare' (vol. 3, p. 40); that he was not 'in a normal state of moral awareness' (*ibid.*); that he was acting 'quite out of character', not 'in his right mind'; that 'one almost expects Onegin to wake (as Tatiana does) and realise that it has all been a dream' (vol. 3, p. 41). All of this is questionable but most dubious of all are the references to a dreamlike state. First, it is impossible that Onegin had somehow heard of Tatyana's nightmare and then proceeded to act out its grisly prediction. Between the dream and the duel there is no connection which may be said to impinge on Onegin's behaviour. Beyond that, it is not true to suggest that the atmosphere of the duel is somehow dreamlike. Quite the reverse. The world of Tatyana's dream has been left behind. We have moved from an unreal universe to a world of stark reality. John Fennell puts it well when referring to the famous stanza in which the weapons are prepared (six, XXIX), which he describes as 'the astonishingly down-to-earth pistol-loading scene' (*Nineteenth-century Russian Literature*, p. 43). No one could mistake these actions, characters and incidents for fantasy or illusion.

The other suggestions advanced by Nabokov present more complications, if only because he covers so much territory, suggesting *non sequiturs* in characterisation, lapses in ethical conduct, and even something close to temporary insanity. The best way of disproving these ideas is to demonstrate that Onegin's behaviour is logical and consistent throughout, which does seem to be the case. We must continue to work back through the events. Immediately preceding the duel came the challenge. In accepting it Onegin demonstrates a dogged determination to victimise Lensky and to ignore any other possible solutions to the crisis, the very attitude which was to characterise the duel itself. This is seen at its clearest in the brief debate which Onegin holds with himself concerning Lensky's challenge. Onegin, who must have suspected that the challenge was on its way, did not think twice before accepting it. Only after Zaretsky had left with his 'always ready' response does Onegin consider the arguments for and against fighting a duel. The argument against comes first, spread out over more than a stanza. Unwound into prose, it runs as follows:

... on strict analysis, calling himself to secret judgement, he had much to accuse himself of. First, it had been wrong of him to make fun so casually of timid, tender love as he had done the previous evening. And second, let the poet fool around; you can forgive that in an eighteen-year-old. Eugene, who loved the young lad with all his heart, ought to show himself to be no playball of prejudices, no ardent boy, no butcher, but a real man of honour and good sense.   (six, X)

He could have disclosed his feelings instead of bristling like a beast; he ought to have disarmed the young man's heart ...   (six, XI)

The arguments are powerful and so lucidly presented that for a moment we could almost expect sanity and decency to prevail. Onegin actually accepts responsibility for what has happened and spells out what must now be done; he must act with honour and good sense. What counter-arguments can there be? But the rest of the discussion is a let-down. The best that Onegin can muster is the squalid idea that it is now too late, because Zaretsky will gossip and public opinion will hold him in contempt (six, XI). This is intrinsically a weak argument compared with the previous one; it is particularly inappropriate in a man who holds society in such contempt. On other occasions he has flouted convention at will; ironically, he will do so again during the duel itself. The important point about this little debate, however, is that its outcome was decided in advance. By sending Zaretsky away and then considering the rights and wrongs of the situation Onegin makes it virtually impossible to free Lensky from the trap. Onegin is hardly going to run after Zaretsky and say that he has changed his mind. At this stage of the affair it seems that Onegin is motivated not by a slavish sense of conformity but by some deep psychological impulse which drives him to continue the process that he has already started.

The hounding of Lensky began the previous day at Tatyana's name-day celebrations. Lensky has pressed Onegin into attending on the understanding that there will not be many people there; as it happens the two young men turn up at a substantial family feast. That is the full extent of Lensky's crime — to have misinformed Onegin, in all innocence. He will die for having done so. What really disconcerts Onegin is the fact that he is plunged into an embarrassing situation by being placed opposite Tatyana. Fresh from her nightmare, she is in a nervous state and can scarcely control herself. It is interesting to note that she does just manage to do so, and Onegin does not have to take part in any distressing or scandalous scene; the all-round embarrassment is soon covered up. Nevertheless, Onegin is infuriated and goes into a huff. He can think only of vengeance against Lensky, even though Lensky has done very little that needs to be avenged. One is struck by the lack of proportion between the young lad's peccadillo and the relentless fury with which Onegin determines to punish it. It is important to remember that at this stage Onegin cannot be considered a victim of society, convention, fate or anything else. He is fully in charge of events; it is he who decides what to do. He could have elected to sulk, get drunk, attempt a seduction; most obviously, if he did not like the crowd he could have made an excuse and left early. Instead he does something quite dramatic; at the ball he monopolises Olga and flirts with her ostentatiously. The seriousness of this must be stressed; Lensky's challenge is not an overreaction. As Nabokov says, 'Lenski's course of action, far from being a temperamental extravaganza, is the only logical course an honourable man could have taken in that set in those times' (vol. 3, p. 16). Onegin had many choices; Lensky had none. Onegin's conduct at the ball, incidentally, flies in the face of convention, invites gossip and impugns his own honour in a manner which suggests that he has little concern for such considerations. Can a man who acts with such forthright independence this evening be seriously considered thirty-six hours later to be an automaton controlled by the forces of convention?

Reviewing the entire succession of events, one is impressed not by any aberrations in Onegin's character or conduct, but by their consistency. They are consistent within themselves and with what we know of Onegin from his previous history. He is selfish, amoral, destructive and predatory. It is not as though he suddenly turns into a monster at the ball and for the duration of the duel; his behaviour was always monstrous. The persecution of Lensky, despite the superficial friendliness which seemed to exist between them, was prefigured. We have referred above to the first visit of Onegin to the Larin household and the conversation which took place immediately after it. Onegin's hounding of Lensky is clearly evident at this early stage. Nabokov, ironically, understands this well. Referring to the actual challenge issued by Lensky on 13 January 1821, he says, 'it is indeed a wonder that the young Lenski had had enough self-control not to send Onegin a cartel of defiance (*lettre d'appel*) [i.e., challenge him to a duel] immediately after the latter's vulgar remarks about mediocre Madonnas and round moons half a year earlier' (vol. 3, p. 16).

Why did he do it?

The question of Onegin's motivation cannot be settled with certainty, though one line of speculation suggests itself, being as satisfying as it is obvious. Onegin cannot endure the sight of such happiness in a young intelligent man. Lensky is rich, handsome, virile but, most of all, transported by his naive love for Olga. He lives most of the time in a state of ecstasy, alternating with bouts of anguish which will be swept away by yet another wave of bliss at the next glimpse of his beloved. Onegin has always lived by the intellect rather than the emotions. He has never known this kind of happiness and he is further away from it when he meets Lensky than he has ever been. This is by no means the only difference between them. In Lensky he meets his direct opposite. Pushkin has summed this up for us in a famous comparison.

> They came together. Wave and stone,
> Poetry and prose, ice and flame
> Were never so different from one another.   (two, XIII)

To this we might add the polarisation between day and night, or light and darkness with which the two were associated in an earlier chapter. In fact, any polarisation will be appropriate in the case of these two men. Under normal circumstances this would be unimportant. The two might have ignored each other or worked out some tolerant form of accommodation. This is what appears to happen between Onegin and Lensky, but that turns out to be a superficial impression. We ought to have known that Onegin's tolerance of Lensky was false. It does not fit in with what we know of him from the first chapter. If Nabokov really wished to find something 'out of character' this is what he should have settled on. Onegin's smiling condescension hides burning envy of the young man's happiness. Not far below that lurks the destructive spirit that we know so well in Onegin. Matter has encountered anti-matter; sooner or later the former will be annihilated.

At first Onegin was content to await the satisfaction of seeing Lensky's emotional castles crumble, which he knew they must do one day:

> And he thought: foolish of me to interfere with
> His momentary rapture;
> Without me the time will come;
> In the meantime let him live on
> And believe in the perfection of the world.   (two, XV)

But as time went by Lensky showed no sign of losing his annoying belief in perfection. On the contrary, with his wedding only a few days away, he was beginning to ascend new summits of happiness. His youthful excitement is something to behold at the end of chapter four. He chatters away to Onegin about Olga, indicating the sensuous beauty which is now emerging in her. On and on he goes in his innocent happiness:

> He was merry. For two weeks hence
> The happy date was set.
> And the mystery of the marriage bed
> And the sweet garland of love
> Awaited his transports of delight ...
>
> He was loved ... or at least
> He thought he was and he was happy.   (four, L and LI)

It was in the midst of all this talk of happiness that Lensky issued, parenthetically, the invitation for Onegin to come to Tatyana's name-day celebrations. This, surely, was the real offence which Onegin felt impelled to avenge: the crime of unlimited happiness.

At some subconscious level — we are not suggesting a deliberate plan — Onegin decides that it is no good waiting for Lensky's absurd bliss to founder on the rocks of real life. Letting him live on is no longer appropriate; he must be destroyed. All of the events occurring at the ball and during the next two days show him relentlessly cornering Lensky and moving in for the kill. He takes one logical step after another, provoking the unavoidable challenge, accepting it immediately, dismissing any qualms with spurious argument, piling further insults on the young man by arriving late, which also raises his own chances of success from very high to near certainty, hurrying him into action lest the inward voice of protest be heard, taking aim early and yet waiting until the last moment — when he sees Lensky beginning to raise his pistol — before administering the *coup de grâce*. How appropriate is Pushkin's description of the immediate aftermath:

> Thus, slowly down the mountainside ...
> A great block of snow descends.
> Deluged with instant cold,
> Onegin rushes up to the young man ...
> He is no more ...
> The fire on the altar has gone out.   (six, XXXI)

The ice has proved too strong for the flame and has put it out.

The concept of Onegin's destructive jealousy serves another useful purpose. Without it Tatyana's colourful nightmare takes some explaining. It is easy enough to understand why Tatyana should dream about Onegin, link him with monsters, set him up as a dominating figure, and so on. What is awkward to assimilate is her prediction of Lensky's violent end at the hands of his 'friend'. This is taken care of if we imagine Tatyana, with her peculiar sensitivity, picking up the faint signals of danger which may have emanated from Onegin. Other people may not have noticed and Tatyana herself did not understand them consciously, but somehow she sensed both the hidden envy of Onegin and the destructive force that accompanied it. This explanation, although admittedly not provided by Pushkin in the text itself, has the advantage of fitting the nightmare, with all its weird and wonderful poetry, into the scheme of things with full plausibility.

The consistency of the present argument extends, incidentally, to the later attitude of Eugene Onegin. At first sight this may not seem to be the case since there is mention of his contrition. If his determination to get rid of Lensky had been so deep-seated, surely he would not feel all that regretful afterwards? One answer to this objection might be that the actual murder brought home to him the full horrific impact of what he had done; the shock brought him to his senses and from then on his reactions were what we might describe as normal. But there is a better answer. Just as his apparent remorse *before* the duel turned out to be spurious because he still had every intention of going through with it (six, X–XI), so is his subsequent contrition flawed. It has no genuine ring to it. This point has been made by James Forsyth. 'There is no doubt here that Pushkin *tells* us that Onegin was haunted by the memory of the duel, but the effect is rather superficial and unsustained ... In short we do not receive a *poetic* impression of Onegin's mood of remorse as we do, for instance, of Tatyana's love for Onegin or of Lensky's feelings between the challenge and the duel' ('Pisarev, Belinsky and Yevgeniy Onegin', p. 172).

All of which is to say, then, that there is nothing very mysterious about Onegin's behaviour. It does not need explaining in terms of outside forces bearing down upon the hero. Fate, society and its conventions, historical circumstances, literary precedents, *mal du siècle* – all or any of these may have some relevance to what goes on but they do not have to be invoked for the formation of an all-embracing exegesis. We do not have to falsify certain details to make ourselves feel more comfortable, like Nabokov who tries to change Lensky's age, or Tchaikovsky who, in his opera, adds a little extra motivation to Onegin's decision to flirt with Olga, by arranging for him to overhear some malicious gossip about himself. Above all we do not have to pretend that the duel does not matter very much because the real interest belongs to Onegin's relationship with Tatyana. What we must do is resist the clever blandishments of our poet-narrator, who disguises Onegin's motivation as well as the gravity of his conduct, and the pressure of inherited opinion which has tended to defend Onegin's reputation by mitigation of his guilt.

One final question arises. If the preceding argument is sound, how can it be that no one has seen it before? Do we really have to fly in the face of all previous critical assessments? As it happens, a single critic stands out for having advanced a view of Onegin similar to the present one. In his essay, 'The strange case of Pushkin and Nabokov', Edmund Wilson confronts Nabokov head on, claiming that 'He does not seem to be aware that Onegin ... is ... decidedly злой − that is, nasty, *méchant* ... There are no out-of-character actions in *Evgeni Onegin*. Nabokov has simply not seen the point' ('The strange case of Pushkin and Nabokov', p. 224). The pity is that Wilson's argument, which shines out like a beacon in a half-lit world, was expressed in fewer than three hundred words and lost in a much larger argument between the two men. It has since been disregarded.

Chapter 5

It is in verse, but is it a novel?

Eugene Onegin claims on its title page to be a 'novel in verse'. The verse, in a literal sense, speaks for itself; but can the work be properly described as a novel? First we are faced with the *de facto* acceptance of this appellation by all readers and critics over a century and a half. Some of the most rewarding essays on *Onegin* are to be found in histories of the Russian *novel* (as our bibliography indicates). Then we must remember the peculiar standing of this work in the dynasty of Russian literature; it is the novelists who look back on it as their revered patriarch. (We shall return to this point). Finally we must take account of the author's intentions. From the outset he described his work as a novel and, despite admitting that it would be 'something like' Byron's *Don Juan*, he was always eager to dissociate the two poetic narratives. Mirsky has summarised the three differences between them: unlike *Don Juan*, *Eugene Onegin* is direct rather than satirical, realistic and contemporary rather than dressed up in semi-Romantic fancifulness, and a work of integrated form and meaning, 'a complete whole, with a beginning, a middle, and an end' (*Pushkin*, p. 141). (It is also much superior in the quality of its poetry but that need not concern us now). But the real distinction is one of density and seriousness. The admiring descendants of this novel are animated by something of substance, something more than the charm and exquisite sense of form which first strike the eye. In attempting to discover what this is we must look for sufficient quality in the ideas and implications of *Eugene Onegin* for us to claim it as a work in which 'the greatest powers of the mind are displayed.' This well known definition of the novel, from Jane Austen's *Northanger Abbey*, is accompanied by a longer one: 'some work in which the most thorough knowledge of human nature, the happiest delineation of its varieties, the liveliest effusions of wit and humour are conveyed to the world in the best chosen language' (chapter five). Such tests as these, when applied to Pushkin's story, do seem to justify its inclusion in the ranks of serious literature rather than pleasurable entertainment. We must conclude by examining the powers of the mind and the knowledge of human nature displayed by *Eugene Onegin*.

'The careless fruit of my amusements'

Pushkin does not invite us to do so. In the first words of the poem, its Dedication, he adopts the stance of a humble journeyman offering the unworthy results of his toil to a nobler recipient. He tells us that his work, 'The careless fruit of my amusements', is not worth the attention of a man of 'fine soul' or 'high thoughts'. This may be conventional modesty but it is also a typically Pushkinian disclaimer. Rarely does our Russian poet seem to be serious; he almost always pretends to be a dealer in flippancy. But his work is full of false signals, and this is one of them. By renouncing all seriousness in advance, and sustaining an impression of levity throughout, he places all the emphasis on easy entertainment and aesthetic delight. These are, in fact, the foremost qualities of *Eugene Onegin* and they provide the flavour of the work, which remains delectable, even though the subject matter oscillates between banality and tragedy. However, they do not preclude seriousness of purpose.

This seriousness may be rather difficult to pin down, but it is there, hiding behind the dismissive frivolity. One of the reasons for its elusiveness is the sheer uncertainty of what is being said. Pushkin's universe is ruled by irony, paradox and oxymoron; apparent contradictions coexist in it without destroying each other. The reader will have to guard against ambiguity and sometimes error. It is not uncommon for critics to arrive at antithetical views of the novel. One will call it sombre and serious, another will say that it is never sombre. One will say that it ends in tragedy, another will claim that there is nothing depressing about the ending. Sometimes, as we have seen, mistakes are made. Another good example concerns the tone of the novel which has often been said to change from youthful ebullience at the beginning to melancholy reflectiveness in chapter eight. A careful reading of the first chapter will show that this is not the case. Most of the boisterous stanzas are located in the first third of the chapter and they are greatly outnumbered by their opposites, stanzas of bile, misanthropy, sadness, regret and near despair. The change in tone occurs *within* the first chapter rather than between it and the last one. And so it goes on. *Eugene Onegin* must be seen as a breeding ground for double meanings and misconceptions. Once accustomed to this concept we can look through the light-heartedness with confident hope of discovering earnest purpose and serious achievement.

An educated pen

The word 'careless' (*nebrezhnyy*) is used again by Pushkin when he is signing off at the end of the novel. He refers to what he has written as these 'careless stanzas' (eight, XLIX) and imagines that the reader can have discovered in the novel little more than relaxation, a few living images, a joke or two and some grammatical mistakes. It all sounds so casual and superficial, the winding down of an easy bit of reading. Not so; the preceding work has actually been quite the opposite – carefully constructed, skilfully executed and full of important ideas.

Pushkin pretends that his work is entirely undemanding. This is an illusion. Only a cultivated reader could have followed the educated pen that traced these five thousand easy-flowing lines. For a start he or she will need a sound education in the classics. He is expected to recognise a dryad when he hears of one, and in this text he will encounter also a bacchante, cupid, nereid and nymph, to say nothing of a muse, unnamed or named (Terpsichore, Melpomene, Thalia *et al.*). He should not think, anachronistically, that an armida belongs to their company. He must know his way around eclogues, elegies, epics, epigrams, epodes and epistles. Gods, goddesses and legendary figures appear in frequent references; he ought to know who they are – Aeolus, Apollo, Circe, Cupid, Cyclops, Cynthia, Cypris, Diana, Hesperus, Hymen, Phoebus, Morpheus, Venus, Zeus and the rest. It is assumed that he knows what Aonia, Hellespont, Tauris and Lethe mean and who Cleopatra, Eve, Leander, Paris, Phaedra, Philomela, Prima, Regulus, Remus and Romulus were. Let us hope he is on nodding acquaintance with Homer, Horace, Juvenal, Ovid, Seneca, Theocritus and Virgil; and if he does not know the difference between Apuleius and Cicero he will miss a saucy little joke in the first stanza of chapter eight.

Beyond that, there are in this sophisticated text dozens of references to historical and literary figures, Russian and foreign, past and contemporary. Their names, or those of their works, bespangle the text from start to finish. Their diversity may be glimpsed from the following examples (which exclude all of the numerous Russian references): Albani, Bayle, Bentham, Bichat, Boileau, Bürger, Byron, Chamfort, Chateaubriand, Corneille, Cottin, Dante, Mme de Staël, Didelot, Faublas, Fontenelle, Gabussi, Gibbon, Goethe, Grimm, Herder, Kant, Lafontaine, Malfilâtre, Marmontel, Manzoni, Maturin, Necker, Nodier, Parny, Pradt, Petrarch, Racine, Richardson, Rousseau, Sadi, St Priest, Say, Schiller, Scott, Shakespeare, Smith, Sterne, Tasso, Tissot, Vandyke, Weber, Zadeck.

To this we must add the fact that Pushkin, although not a brilliant linguist, interpolates in his Russian discourse phrases or quotations in English, French, Italian and Latin. He also appends forty-four footnotes which, although they are not particularly serious because of their offhand or ironical manner, nevertheless impart a suggestion of academic seriousness to the novel.

When all of these references and other devices are brought out on parade they look almost pretentious. Is the poet showing off by name-dropping? Is he too proud of his own education? No such impression may be drawn from a reading of *Eugene Onegin*. All of these allusions are absorbed into the text

without effort; nothing obtrudes, unless it is intended to do so by way of a joke. Here is another of the Pushkin paradoxes. This easily-told story is stuffed full of enriching references the like of which only a cultivated and patient reader can competently cope with. So much for the self-confessed carelessness. This is a solid and scrupulous narrative, which taunts the reader and tests him. You are at liberty to ignore all the mischievous invocations and get on with the story, if that is what you prefer. But by doing so you risk the poet's contempt for your lack of discernment; he expects you to chase after them, and to take delight in doing so, from Zeus in the second stanza to Sadi in the penultimate one.

In search of the serious content

Eugene Onegin is so busy pretending not to be important that, even if we are inclined to look through its frivolity in search of the serious content, we cannot be sure of what we are confronted with. Most readers eventually come to the conclusion that there is something of consequence to be discovered in the story, but there is much room for debate about what this is. It will be clear from the earlier chapters that the present argument is built upon suspicion of widespread misconceptions about the plot, the events and the characters of this novel. These misconceptions may be shown to extend also to its deeper meanings. At the risk of brief recapitulation we must define again the areas where mistakes appear to have been made and then make new suggestions about the ultimate significance of *Eugene Onegin*.

Privacy of conscience and moral awareness

These phrases are borrowed from Richard Freeborn (*Rise of the Russian Novel*, p. 37). They are meant to apply to Tatyana, who is taken by this critic and many another to embody the qualities referred to. But they do not quite fit the heroine whom we have been discussing above. If Tatyana was not really tempted to yield to Onegin, as our argument

has suggested, she cannot be credited with a high degree of conscience-stricken morality. This does not mean, however, that conscience and morality play no part in our understanding of the novel. In fact they remain, or ought to remain, foremost among the reader's preoccupations. It is only by reconsidering the misbehaviour and moral responsibility of the characters that we get anywhere near the blurred truth of *Eugene Onegin*. For this to happen we must ask the right questions and accept awkward answers if they seem to be true. What is the most important event in the novel? Surely not the double failure of a possible love match, but the death of Lensky. Who was responsible for it? Surely no-one other than Eugene Onegin himself. The novel does have much to teach us about the privacy of conscience and moral responsibility, but the vehicle for this kind of ethical instruction must be not Tatyana but Onegin. By careful consideration of what he does, and why he does it, we can learn a good deal about the outer reaches of selfishness and the need for restraint and discipline in human behaviour. He is, as a character, so plausible and consistent that the urgent need for moral self-control, a quality of which he has no sense at all, emerges with clarity and insistence.

History and fate

The incorrect idea that *Eugene Onegin* has much to tell us about the mysterious workings of history or fate need not detain us long. The novel has sometimes been viewed as a work of primarily social and political significance. This approach − even if it be true in part − may be disregarded here, for two reasons. First, there is a wealth of material already available on the subject; it has probably had too generous a run for its money. Second, this kind of emphasis serves to distort and diminish the true quality of *Eugene Onegin*, which should be seen as European and universal rather than essentially Russian. The hero and his conduct are of interest not because of circumstances peculiar to Russia in the 1820−30s. They are of significance to lovers of European letters in general

and, beyond that, to all readers of good literature who care to reflect on the psychological and ethical implications of what they have read. You are at liberty to assess and enjoy this novel as a picture of Russia or as a universal masterpiece, or both at the same time, but the greatest benefit will derive from the broadest definition of what it may be said to have achieved.

If this is true of the historical and political content, it applies with greater strength to the concept of fate which, as we have seen, has also haunted *Onegin* criticism. Again, no one can say that this is entirely wrong, but it does seem more interesting and profitable to think of Onegin in terms of his psychology and deficient moral awareness. Only in the vaguest sense can we see him as a hero gripped by outside forces which propel him to an ineluctably tragic end. In the course of the story he has too much freedom of action for this to be really true and, in any case, at the end of it there is no piercing sense of tragedy. Let us concentrate not on any external forces, but on the man himself, his mind and his unprincipled misbehaviour. The workings of Fate and History do not provide *Eugene Onegin* with its deepest meanings.

The possibility and closeness of happiness

Probably the most searching question raised by the novel concerns the prospect of human happiness. Tatyana says sadly at the end, 'But happiness was so possible, so close!' (eight, XLVII). In so far as this concerns her relationship with the hero this is a misconception, but at least it shows up one of her main preoccupations. Like all of us, she wants to be happy. So did Alexander Pushkin, though he almost never was. In one famous lyric ('It's time, my friend, it's time ...' (1834)) he claims that 'There is no happiness on earth, though there are tranquillity and freedom.' Throughout *Onegin* he pursues the quest for happiness and his failure to achieve it, for himself or for his major characters, appears to confirm this dismal conclusion.

And yet things turn out to be more complicated than this.

Pushkin manages to demonstrate the unattainability of happiness for people of a certain kind and with certain attitudes, but he also suggests that other personalities and other attitudes might gain access to this elusive state. His own unhappiness comes first. Even in the early stages of the story his voice rings with sadness. His youth has gone and he is unhappy about it. The self-applied adjectives in the nineteenth stanza are revealing: 'sad', 'anguished', 'disappointed', 'indifferent', plus the transferred epithets 'tedious' and 'alienated' which appear to be directed at the stage but obviously refer back to the narrator. Add the word 'unspeaking' and the total comes to seven negative pronouncements in a dozen lines, a most emphatic statement of unhappiness. The impression is that of a man entering middle age and regretting the passing of his youth (though Pushkin was only twenty-four at the time of writing). He has lost the sense of joy and desire (one, XXIX); he has ruined his life, become sad and grown cold (one, XXX); his happiness has disappeared like footprints on the meadow (one, XXXI).

This litany of personal wretchedness turns out to be only the preamble to an even sorrier story. Eugene Onegin is in a worse state. He has everything anyone could apparently wish for, including wealth and unlimited leisure. Behind him lies a recent history of amorous conquest on the grand scale and when we encounter him his life consists in going about from one entertainment to another. Yet Pushkin feels impelled to ask the question, 'But was he happy?' and to answer it with an emphatic 'No' (one, XXXVI–XXXVII). It soon turns out that Onegin suffers from a form of unhappiness so acute that it is best thought of as an affliction or ailment (one, XXXVIII). All the trouble that is to come will stem from his present state of coldness, alienation and boredom.

In all of this there is a useful reminder of the difference between temporary pleasure and lasting contentment, but boredom is the key word. Boredom lies at the root of Onegin's unhappiness and its depiction gives us the clearest warning of the wrong way to live a life. It also marks the difference between him and Pushkin, whose own misery is not based on this negative quality. The poet sees this himself. In a typically offhand and jocular couple of stanzas (one, LIV–LV) he informs us that, whereas Onegin relapses into boredom after giving rural life no more than two days to impress or amuse him, he, Pushkin, is a great country-lover. Onegin is bored always, everywhere and with everything; it is his practice to anticipate boredom by yawning his way into all new circumstances and enterprises.

Perhaps the strongest message to emerge from the career of this unlovable hero is that boredom is a great crime against humanity and against life. Pushkin puts it obliquely but nevertheless with clarity. The worst thing you can do with existence, his novel implies, is to be bored with it. Life is not easy for anyone. For most people it is truly difficult to manage. Above all, by promising more than it can deliver in the way of happiness, significance, freedom and permanence, life is deeply disappointing. But it cannot and must not be ignored or forgotten, rejected or simply slept through. It is to be endured when necessary, noticed and wondered at always, and whenever possible celebrated. Taken overall, *Eugene Onegin* is a great celebration of the bits and pieces that messily go to make up human existence. In its foreground we watch people struggling for contentment and making things very difficult for themselves, but there is a strong sense of ordinary life proceeding enjoyably behind them. The unnamed characters and creatures in the background do not know the meaning of the word boredom. The ballet lovers admire Istomina (one, XX); the girl from Okhta fetches her milk (one, XXXV); the red-footed goose slides out on the pond (four, XLII); the young boy serves cream to go with the tea (three, XXXVII); the peasant lad plays with his sledge and his dog (five, II). Meanwhile for us readers cheerful rainbow patterns decorate the city pavement on a dark evening (one, XXVII); the bees start their business in early spring (seven, I); the sun plays on blocks of blue ice along the Neva (eight, XXXIX); the deserted lake is a pleasure to walk along (one, LV); captivating sounds float across the night air (one, XLVIII); beautiful flurries of snow whirl past in the morning sunshine (six, XXXIV); Onegin's castle looks out on to a lovely vista of meadows, flowers, cattle and half-hidden hamlets (two, I). By recording all of these details, albeit in an unspectacular manner, Pushkin registers a degree of satisfaction amounting at times to scarcely repressible joy. Life is there to be lived and enjoyed, in the city and the country, the morning and the evening, the autumn and the spring; to be bored with it is the ultimate mistake.

Dealing with death

The accumulation of loving detail is the redeeming feature of *Eugene Onegin* as far as the story-telling is concerned. The narrative itself is particularly bleak. Its main characters are studies in discontent. The happiness of Lensky and Olga is derided and short-lived. Promising occasions, like the name-day celebration, are soured by unfortunate incidents. No one actually achieves anything (except Pushkin by his writing). And, worst of all, we are never very far away from thoughts of death. They are there in the first stanza, when Onegin wishes his dying relative into the arms of the devil, and in the last one, in which Pushkin celebrates the idea of dying young: 'Blessed is he who has left the feast of life early without draining his goblet of wine to the bottom . . .' (eight, LI). Numerous deaths come in between. Onegin is careless enough to lose two relatives, father and uncle, in as many stanzas (one, LI, LII), though the sadness is neutralised by the funeral feast which is described hilariously in only eight lines of the next one (a splendid example of Pushkin's laconic expressiveness). Dmitri Larin goes to his grave in the second chapter and, as he does so, ensures that the last five stanzas are devoted to the theme of death. Pushkin reminds us that it will not be long before our grandchildren squeeze us out of the world; he at least will leave a reputation behind. In the last chapter we hear of the death of Tatyana's beloved nurse, while the middle of the novel is dominated by the demise of Lensky, something altogether more serious. He dies a multiple death. His murder is sensationally prefigured in chapter five, ruthlessly depicted in chapter six and apparently recalled every day by Onegin, as we learn in chapter eight. The deaths are many and varied. More often than not they are given light-hearted treatment, but the odour of human mortality pervades *Eugene Onegin* from first to last.

This being so, it is all the more surprising that every last reader remembers the novel as enjoyable and life-enhancing. The paradox is peculiarly Pushkinian. His remarkable achievement is to have told the saddest of stories in affirmative terms. The same sort of thing can be found in Shakespeare. In *As You Like It*, for example, Jaques tells us about the seven ages of man, making each one of them sound unpleasant. The infant mewls, the schoolboy whines and creeps, the lover sighs, the soldier curses, the justice stares severely, and the last two ages are nothing more than decay leading to oblivion. Yet, even as depicted here, life, with its compensations, does not seem all that bad, and these are among the best-loved lines in English poetry. The poetry is a key factor in both cases; exquisitely-used language is in itself an assertion of beauty and goodness. In Pushkin's case the poison of death is neutralised also by a light touch, an ironic manner and the continual reassertion of life's simple delights by means of the pleasurable details to which we have drawn attention.

We must give final emphasis to this point by reminding ourselves of Onegin's inability to appreciate the delightful minutiae of the everyday world. The two stanzas which we examined in detail in chapter 1 showed Onegin to be an expert in the field of missing out. Good conversation, reading, writing, the rich offerings of the countryside, the nicer parts of city life, interesting people and the better qualities of ordinary folk, all these possibilities for deepening experience and achieving warmth or consolation are by-passed with a yawn, dismissed without a thought, or simply not noticed. Miserable Eugene Onegin: it is his lot to sleep, not when the world has relapsed into dullness, but when the loveliest things in creation emerge to mock him for his foolish inattentiveness. Pushkin's message to us is clear, even if he himself could not live up fully to his own prescription. Death should be forgotten, laughed at or welcomed lightly when it comes. Before it does there is much to be done, much to be seen, heard and experienced. Wonderment and awe should never be far away; a surprised red-footed goose skidding across an icy pond is a glorious little miracle, enough to dispel all doubt and induce a sense of real happiness with the world that exists.

Knowledge of human nature

Another of the substantial differences between *Eugene Onegin* and Byron's *Don Juan* is to be sensed through the solidity of characterisation in the former. Pushkin has created in this work the very first group of properly authenticated modern Russian characters, credible people who are fascinating to observe, both individually and in interaction. (The longest sections of this study have been assigned to this subject because of its importance). The author's contribution to our knowledge of human nature is substantial both in itself and as the initiation of a new literary method suitable for subsequent development on a broad scale.

Arising from the characters and their conduct are all of the ideas and implications which we have just discussed. This is the great merit of the novel, beyond its technical achievement as Russia's finest piece of sustained poetry. For all its disavowal of serious purposes, in practice it does demand close attention and it does provoke thought. There is a lot of Pushkinian wisdom in this story. The poet has much to tell us about genuine moral responsibility, conscience and self-discipline, about the ways in which happiness should and should not be sought or relationships should and should not be formed, about useful and useless attitudes to human life and the death in which it must end. All of these thoughts must remain, stirring, in the mind of an attentive reader, though he may have some difficulty in perceiving them through the haze set up by the aesthetic charm of this clever creation. Pushkin's abiding interest in the foolishness of much human conduct is what provides the solid content of *Eugene Onegin*. It will stand up to innumerable re-readings, each one of which is increasingly likely to deepen the impression that behind all the entertainment the powers of an acute mind and a creative intelligence are indeed on display.

Eugene Onegin as a landmark

The full quality of *Eugene Onegin* is hidden from those who cannot read Russian; because of its poetry it is the least translatable of all the world's novels. Even through translation, however, it should be identifiable as a prominent landmark in European culture. A work of intrinsic high quality and originality, it also marks the beginning of change on a massive scale and points to a new future for Russian letters. Within fifty years of Pushkin's death his successors were to reach out into Europe and America, turning his revered heritage, in which *Eugene Onegin* plays a central part, into sovereign literary attainment.

In chapter 1 some indication was given of Alexander Pushkin's significance as a linguistic innovator. This achievement is endorsed by the eminent Russian linguist G. O. Vinokur in a discussion entitled 'The creation of the national standard language', which demonstrates that no other individual had a greater impact on the development of Russian. 'It was in Pushkin,' Vinokur concludes, 'that the national language achieved the standard to which all the complex development ... from the end of the seventeenth century had tended' (*The Russian Language: a Brief Study*, p. 125). Since *Eugene Onegin* is the richest efflorescence of Pushkin's Russian, it is clear that this novel actually had a determining influence upon the very tongue in which it was written.

In literary terms the novel is hardly less of an epoch-maker. It is an amazing hybrid, born of a Classical spirit in a Romantic age, its disciplined elegance cohabiting with subversive freedom of discourse. This is the first credible, modern Russian narrative in the reading of which no allowances have to be made, no exaggerations apologised for, no serious gaffes and lapses accommodated. For the first time Russian readers are dealing with reality; the setting is now and here, the descriptions are lucidity itself. In the words of F. D. Reeve, 'Pushkin's *Eugene Onegin* divides the improbable novel from the probable, speaking both historically and artistically' (*The Russian Novel*, p. 14).

For the first time in Russian literature the story recedes in importance and the characters step forward, fully authenticated, to take over the main interest. The plot of *Eugene Onegin* is so unsensational that it verges upon the uneventful, and is frequently described as such. The shift of emphasis from exciting story to fascinating character is one of the reasons why the murder of Lensky − the only remarkable incident in the novel − should be so easily forgotten and so often overlooked. It also explains the fact that, although the ending may be regarded in one sense as unsatisfactory, because it resolves nothing and seems to peter out on a disappointing down beat, the work as a whole may not be dismissed as ill-conceived or unsuccessful. Events turn out to be as inconclusive as they often are in real life; people are shown to be more interesting. Later Russian writers, beginning almost immediately with Lermontov (whose 'hero', Pechorin, imitates Onegin in being named after a river) will follow this model in droves.

They will also continue a particular tradition here established by Pushkin, that of the unheroic hero ranged against a more likeable and self-assured heroine. Ineffectual men and assertive women, appearing together or separately, will thickly populate the pages of Russian fiction soon to come and their supply will not have dried up even in the days of Chekhov and Gorky. (Concerning the subsequent strong heroines the debate still continues as to whether these fictional creatures, deriving from Tatyana, merely reflected their many real-life counterparts − the Decembrist wives, Vera Zasulich, Sofya Perovskaya, and others − or whether they may have served somehow as an inspirational force for them). Above all, the hallmark of Russian literature will be a study of human nature and psychology. The formation of character, the interaction between individuals, the motivation of misconduct and the repercussions which follow from it − these aspects of the human condition, which assume the highest significance for the first time in *Eugene Onegin* − are shortly to become the focus of interest (as opposed to superficial entertainment or sensationalism), in Turgenev, Tolstoy, Dostoyevsky and most other Russian writers of consequence. The reputations and impact of such artists in

Europe are well enough known now to speak for themselves; in some measure they all descend from Pushkin. When, subsequently, debts are acknowledged by Henry James or Flaubert to Turgenev, by James Joyce to Lermontov, by Kafka to Dostoyevsky and by Orwell to Zamyatin, these writers will be trading against an account opened by Pushkin. Having himself drawn on Shakespeare, Sterne, Scott and Byron, he then left behind rich deposits for the benefit of his fellow countrymen. Pushkin stands in the middle of the east—west literary market-place, and in the centre of his stall stands *Eugene Onegin*.

Thus the far-reaching effects of this appealing work can scarcely be overvalued. It set its clear, deep stamp upon the Russian language and on Russian letters in such a way as to determine the very course of European culture and in a manner given to very few works of literature. In doing so it found an appropriate destiny, since this work, which at first sight seems to be peculiarly Russian is, in fact, not merely a national landmark but a product of, and a contribution to, European civilisation. In its loving and scrupulous tending of artistic form, its technical excellence and its avoidance of extremism and outlandishness it belongs as much to Paris, Vienna and London as it does to Moscow. The trouble is that, in order to appreciate the fullness of this truth, educated non-Russian Europeans will have to work hard at an accessible but rather complicated foreign language. One thing may be said in all seriousness: anyone who takes the trouble to learn Russian in order to read Pushkin, and to feast on the riches of *Eugene Onegin*, will have spent the time well and will never regret it.

Guide to English translations and further reading

Translations

Given the difficulty of the undertaking it is surprising to discover that the whole of *Eugene Onegin* was translated into English verse, using rhymed iambic tetrameters and a fourteen-line stanza, no fewer than seven times in the century between 1881 and 1977. The translations are as follows:

Eugene Onegin, translated by Lt. Col. T. Spalding, Macmillan, London, 1881.

Eugene Onegin, translated by Babette Deutsch in *The Works of Alexander Pushkin*, selected and edited by Avrahm Yarmolinsky, Random House, New York, 1936. Revised, augmented and re-published by Penguin Books, Harmondsworth, Middlesex, 1964.

Eugene Onegin, translated by Dorothea Prall Radin and George Z. Patrick, University of California Press, Berkeley, 1937.

Evgeny Onegin, translated by Oliver Elton, The Pushkin Press, London, 1937.

Eugene Onegin, translated by Walter Arndt, Dutton, New York, 1963.

Eugene Onegin, translated by Eugene Kayden, Yellow Strings, Ohio, 1964.

Eugene Onegin, translated by Charles Johnston, Scolar Press, Ilkley, Yorkshire, 1977. Republished with minor revisions by Penguin Books, 1979.

Equally surprising is the quality of the very first translation, by Lt. Col. Spalding in 1881. Although almost forgotten now, it is remarkably accurate and sensitive. Above all, it reads easily − apart from a few archaisms which have overtaken it with the passage of time − because of the translator's brave decision to stick mainly to masculine (single-syllable) rhymes. Anyone who can locate a copy will be rewarded by a fascinating piece of work. All of the others use feminine rhymes (two-syllable ones like 'sickened/quickened' from Elton's first stanza), Radin and Kayden in parts of the stanza, the others regularly through-out, as in the original. The translation which is at present most readily available, by Charles Johnston, is accurate and serviceable, though the reader will have to disregard the translator's anachronistic decision to drop the capital letters at the line-beginnings. (Capitals have been reinstated on those occasions in chapter 1 when Johnston's translation has been used in quotation). For reasons outlined in chapter 1 no translation transmits anything to its reader beyond the basic story-line and a pallid afterglow of Pushkin's style. *Caveat lector.*

The most famous English version of this novel is *Eugene Onegin*, translated from the Russian with a commentary, in four volumes, by Vladimir Nabokov, Bollingen Foundation, New York, 1964. A controversial work, with its deadly accuracy vitiated by quirky English and a curiously vague iambic plod, this translation is of greatest use to specialists interested in every last nuance of meaning. On the other hand, a feast of European culture is provided in the accompanying notes and commentary, four hundred thousand words of excellent Pushkinian detail, comment and opinion. The many references above to Nabokov relate to this edition.

Books

The following books contain substantial materials on *Eugene Onegin*:

Bayley, J. *Pushkin: A Comparative Study*, Cambridge, 1971.

Boyd, A.F. *Aspects of the Russian Novel*, Totowa, N.J., 1972.

Briggs, A.D.P. *Alexander Pushkin: a Critical Study*, Croom Helm, 1983.

Brown, W.E. *A History of Russian Literature of the Romantic Period*, Ann Arbor, 1986, vol. 3.

Chizhevsky, D. *Evgenij Onegin*, Cambridge, Mass., 1953.

Clayton, J.D. *Ice and Flame: A. Pushkin's 'Eugene Onegin'*, Toronto, 1985.

Fennell, J. *Nineteenth-century Russian Literature: Studies of Ten Russian Writers*, London, 1973.

Freeborn, R. *The Rise of the Russian Novel*, Cambridge, 1973.

Gifford, H. *The Novel in Russia*, London, 1964.

Hoisington, S.S. *Russian Views of Pushkin's 'Eugene Onegin'*, Indiana, 1988.

Lavrin, J. *Pushkin and Russian Literature*, London, 1947.

Mirsky, D.S. *Pushkin*, London, 1926.

Reeve, F.D. *The Russian Novel*, London, 1966.

Richards, D.J. and Cockrell, C.R.S. *Russian Views of Pushkin*, Oxford, 1976.

Scherr, B.P. *Russian Poetry*, California, 1986.

Schmidgall, G. *Literature as Opera*, New York, 1977.

Todd, W.M. *Fiction and Society in the Age of Pushkin*, Cambridge, Mass., 1986.

Vickery, W.N. *Alexander Pushkin*, New York, 1970.

Hundreds of articles have been written about *Eugene Onegin*. Here is a select list of some which are particularly useful:

Clayton, J. D. 'New directions in Soviet criticism on *Evgenii Onegin*', *Canadian Slavonic Papers*, June, 1980, XXII, No. 2, 208–19.
   '*Evgenii Onegin*: Symbolism of time and space', *Russian Language Journal*, 1981, XXXV, No. 120, 43–58.
   'Towards a feminist reading of *Evgenii Onegin*', *Canadian Slavonic Papers*, 1987, XXIX, 255–65.
Clipper-Sethi, R. 'A lesson for novelists; or The dramatic structure of *Evgenij Onegin*', *Russian Literature*, 1983, XIV–XVI, 397–411.
Forsyth, J. 'Pisarev, Belinsky and Yevgeniy Onegin', *Slavonic and East European Review*, 1970, XLVIII, 163–80.
Gregg, R. A. 'Tat'iana's two dreams: the unwanted spouse and the demonic lover', *Slavonic and East European Review*, 1970, LVIII, No. 113, 492–505.
   'Rhetoric in Tat'jana's last speech', *Slavic and East European Journal*, 25, No. 1, 1981, 1–12.
Gustafson, R. F. 'The metaphor of the seasons in *Evgenij Onegin*, *Slavic and East European Journal*, 1962, VI, No. 1, 6–20.
Katz, M. R. 'Dreams in Pushkin', *California Slavic Studies*, 1980, XI, 71–103 (especially 91–102).
Matlaw, R. E. 'The dream in *Yevgeniy Onegin* with a note on *Gore ot Uma*', *Slavonic and East European Review*, 1959, XXXIII, No. 89, 487–503.
Mitchell, S. 'The digressions in *Yevgeniy Onegin*', *Slavonic and East European Review*, 1965, XLIV, 51–65.
Shaw, J. T. 'The problem of unity in the author–narrator's stance in *Evgenij Onegin*', *Russian Language Journal*, 1981, XXXV, No. 120, 25–42.
Simmons, E. J. 'English translations of *Eugene Onegin*', *Slavonic and East European Review*, 1938, XVII, No. 49, 198–208.
Wilson, E. 'The strange case of Pushkin and Nabokov', in *A Window on Russia*, London, 1972, 209–37.
Woodward, J. B. 'The principle of contradictions in *Yevgeniy Onegin*', *Slavonic and East European Review*, 1982, No. 60, 25–43.